AMERICA'S
NATIONAL PARKS

CLB 2777
© 1993 CLB Publishing Ltd., Godalming, Surrey, England.
All rights reserved.
This 1993 edition published by Crescent Books,
distributed by Outlet Book Company, Inc., a Random House Company,
40 Engelhard Avenue, Avenel, New Jersey 07001.
Random House
New York • Toronto • London • Sydney • Auckland
Printed and bound in Hong Kong.
ISBN 0 517 06044 2
8 7 6 5 4 3 2 1

AMERICA'S NATIONAL PARKS

Text by
CHRISTOPHER C. PICK

CRESCENT BOOKS
NEW YORK • AVENEL, NEW JERSEY

Man's traditional attitude – or rather, one should say, the traditional attitude of white, western man – toward the natural world has been one of superiority. Nature in all its manifestations is a resource to be exploited. Trees are felled for their timber; animals are hunted and shot for their skins and their meat; the seas are fished; the ground itself is torn up to gain the rich minerals hidden beneath. The list of depredations is endless. Nor is the damage and destruction merely short-term. Once destroyed, the balance of nature cannot restore itself in the next generation. Polluted rivers and streams stay polluted, and it is the work of decades to restore them to health. The scars across the land made by mining or quarrying take years to heal. And, above all, the delicately poised relationship of living things, the entire ecological balance, can easily be shattered by the exploitation of just one element within that balance.

This may seem a brutal characterization. But in essence it remains a true one. It can still be seen in the cynical and wholesale exploitation of the Amazonian rain forests and the destruction of indigenous communities there; in the proposed construction, now fortunately halted, of a dam in Tasmania on the site of an outstandingly important area for wildlife; in regular over fishing and the consequent destruction of fish stocks. It can be seen too, many people would argue, in nuclear weaponry, a military arsenal that, in spite of easing East-West tensions, still exists, and should it be used, will destroy the natural, and the man-made world, once and for all.

The concept of a national park is in contradiction to the idea that man is at nature's disposal. National parks are founded in two beliefs: that people need substantial areas of the undisturbed, natural world in which to relax and recuperate; and that the natural world must be preserved on its own terms, for its own inherent values. Man's recreation, his literal re-creation; and the conservation of a world that far predates – and will far outlast – every manifestation of man. These two ideas, even though occasionally a little contradictory in practice, are the touchstones of the national park movement around the world. And it is indeed a matter for considerable optimism that in many nations – some 120 at the time of writing – the concept has taken root, has survived and thrives; the more so since in many of these countries very real, if short-term, economic advantage could be derived from exploitation of these areas.

First page: the Grand Canyon – one of the natural wonders of the world – in Grand Canyon National Park, Arizona. Previous page: a spectacular view of the Grand Canyon from Hopi Point. Facing page: Little Pigeon River, in Great Smoky Mountains National Park.

It could be a matter of some surprise as well, that it was in the United States of America that the idea of a national park system originated. The USA is the land par excellence of individual endeavor. More than any other, the nation was created, its very physical boundaries set, by the efforts of many individuals rather than by a collective, centrally directed impetus. Yet in many ways, the national park concept is in total opposition to the ethic of the individual, for the national park concept is founded, and remains almost entirely dependent, on government willingness to act in the common good and withhold land from exploitation.

We may now, with the benefit of hindsight, judge the American frontiersman harshly. The land was exploited for immediate economic gain, without any consideration at all for its long-term good management. Often long-established indigenous Native American communities were humiliated and cheated of their land, their way of life destroyed; and they themselves were expelled or killed. In the Great Smoky Mountains of Tennessee, for instance, the Cherokees could present little resistance to the first European settlers, and in 1828, having lost their land and culture, they were marched off to alien Oklahoma, and much of their land was cleared for agriculture. The start of the 20th century saw the land invaded a second time – by timber companies which, in little more than two decades, stripped the centuries-old forests, felling two-thirds of the trees. Mill towns were built, streams dammed and then released to carry away logs: once fertile soil became a wasteland, prey to fire and erosion.

This is one example of man's rapaciousness. Another is in the sequoia forests of California. Here, in barely forty years – at the end of the nineteenth century – loggers wiped out virtually an entire forest, including many of its finest specimens: trees more than a thousand years old. On a smaller scale, this happened countless times as the frontier was pushed to its westernmost limits.

Yet at the same time, two counter-influences were developing, and they eventually came together to lessen the frontier's rawness. One was literary – found chiefly among East Coast writers and artists. The other originated among some of the early settlers themselves.

Early proponents of the idea of a national park system included George Catlin, who spent much of the 1830s studying the Indians of the far west. In 1841, he produced a two-volume work entitled

Manners of the North American Indians. Others were the botanist William Barter and the celebrated ornithologist John James Audubon. Writers such as James Fenimore Cooper, Ralph Waldo Emerson and Henry David Thoreau all found spiritual refreshment in nature at its most wild, and strongly criticized contemporary, utilitarian values which looked to the land only for economic gain. For them, the survival of wildernesses was a matter of great psychological importance for a land whose character had been so profoundly marked and defined by the very existence of untamed land. This idea took root, and by the 1860s the first practical handbook on conservation, *Man and Nature*, by George Perkins Marsh, had been published.

By no means were all frontier settlers insensitive men, impelled by financial motives alone. The very beauty and isolation of the frontier drew many men to it. They found in the landscape a quality that touched their souls. Such men included the writer and naturalist Enos Mills, who traveled west to the Rocky Mountains in 1884, at the age of fourteen, and devoted many years of his life to campaigning for a national park in the Rocky Mountains. His aim was fulfilled in 1915, when the Rocky Mountain National Park was established. Another celebrated pioneer of the national park movement was John Muir – Scottish born, Wisconsin raised – whose love for the Sierra Nevada led him to press for, and eventually obtain, state and federal protection for the region. Of the threat to the redwoods and giant sequoias of California he once wrote dismissively: "No doubt these trees would make good lumber after passing through a sawmill, just as George Washington after passing through the hands of a French cook would have made good food."

Without the efforts of such people, the first national parks would never have been established. Huge tracts of wilderness, their wildlife and vegetation, would have been lost to the plow, the axe, the miner's shovel – and the nation would have been much the poorer. We owe them a great deal.

In 1870, scarcely more than a century ago, the Yellowstone region of Wyoming and Montana was barely known. A few trappers and prospectors had explored it, but the stories they brought back of its spouting geysers and amazing scenery were dismissed as fanciful travelers' tales. That year, under the leadership of General Henry D. Washburn, surveyor-general of the Montana Territory, an expedition set out to explore the area. What its members saw confirmed those earlier accounts – confirmed them not merely as the truth but, if anything, as over-modest reports of the splendors of the land. Discussions in camp brought forth the idea, thought to have originated from Cornelius Hedges, a Montana judge, that the region should be preserved as a national park for the benefit of the people. A two-year campaign followed, in the Press and in Congress, and in 1872 the world's first national park – the Yellowstone National Park – was established.

Yellowstone was not quite the first region to be set aside for the public's benefit. Eight years earlier, a small part of the Yosemite Valley in California had been similarly dedicated. But the reserve here was tiny; there already existed a flourishing tourist trade and, in any case, control rested with the state authorities, not with the federal government. This area later became part of the much larger Yosemite National Park, which was established in 1890.

Now that it had taken root, the national park concept quickly spread – both within the USA and elsewhere. Setting up its first national park in 1887 – near Banff, Alberta – Canada simply used the wording of the Yellowstone Act. In the USA, four more parks were founded in the 1890s: Yosemite, Sequoia, Mount Rainier and General Grant (now known as Kings Canyon). By the time the National Park Service was formed in 1916 there were sixteen national parks and twenty-one national monuments. Smaller than national parks, national monuments are intended to conserve a single natural feature.

But this is to look some way ahead. In the intervening years some major battles had to be fought. One of the first was in Yellowstone itself. A skeptical Congress had gone along with the idea of a national park, at least partly because it had been convinced that no economic use for the land could be found; there were, after all, frosts in every month of the year. But by 1886 valuable mineral deposits had been located underground, and a proposal was made to build railroad tracks across the park. The issue went to Congress, very much on the lines of the interests of free enterprise and commerce versus the national heritage – and the national heritage won: permission was refused. Two decades later, equal fortune did not attend the argument over Hetch Hetchy; a narrow valley in the Yosemite National Park. San Francisco needed water and proposed to flood the valley, which John Muir considered the equal in beauty of the Yosemite Valley further south. And the San Francisco authorities eventually won.

Set-back though this undoubtedly was (John Muir died of a broken heart), it led directly to the National Park Services Act of 1916, which strengthened and safeguarded the status of National Park territory. Since then the Service has gone from strength to strength and, more importantly, the conservationist philosophy behind it has gained increasing acceptance. However, not total acceptance: in the mid-1950s a battle was necessary to save the Dinosaur National Monument from being submerged by a dam. A few years later, Glen Canyon, which although one of the finest canyons in the nation, but not a protected area, was lost underneath the waters of Lake Powell. And in the mid-1960s a veritable storm of public protest greeted an astounding proposal to construct two dams in the Grand Canyon itself, the very symbol of America's splendid landscape. In 1968 the developers eventually had to admit defeat.

The problems that the national park movement has faced in the last decade are subtler than those of sheer survival, but crucial none the less. The legislation establishing Yellowstone stated that the region was to be "set apart as a public park or pleasuring-ground for the benefit and enjoyment of the people." The Act that set up the National Park Service was worded in similar, though not identical terms: "to conserve the scenery and natural and historic objects and the wildlife therein and to provide ... for the enjoyment of the same ... by such means as will leave them unimpaired for the enjoyment of future generations." While numbers of visitors remained relatively low, these two functions – conservation and public recreation – remained, by and large, compatible. But recent years have brought more and more visitors to the national parks. The most frequently visited park, Great Smoky Mountains, has well over eight million visitors a year; and the ten most popular have no less than 30 million recreational visits a year. Such numbers, welcome though they of course are in many respects, bring many difficulties with them, and the national park administrators have had to develop skills of management and control of people as well as natural resources. To preserve the environment, the number of visitors to parts of many parks are strictly limited. Some areas are designated wilderness areas, which remain strictly undeveloped. Camping permits, and permits issued to backcountry hikers, are rationed; the number of cars entering a park is severely limited, and visitors are encouraged to take to their feet.

The number of visitors is an outward sign of the conflict – sometimes potential, sometimes actual – between recreation and conservation. But, in fact, it goes far deeper. For some decades after 1916, the parks' first priority was tourism. Hotels were built within park boundaries; stores, shops and golf courses encouraged; roads constructed. Even the parks' most precious resources – their wildlife and vegetation – were enlisted as entertainment. In Yellowstone, bears were fed garbage and grandstands were erected for visitors to watch. Spotlights played over "Old Faithful" in the same park. In Yosemite, a fire of logs and bark was pushed every night off Glacier Point – 3,000 feet above the Yosemite Valley.

But slowly attitudes began to change. A biocentrist approach came to predominate – an approach that values the natural landscape and its wildlife for itself, above all else, and one that gives first priority to the preservation of the wild environment on its own terms. Visitors must accept the land as it is. Few concessions are made to their comfort and convenience.

This is surely as it should be. The time scale of the natural world is far, far greater than that of any individual human being. The landscapes of our national parks were being formed millions – often hundreds of millions – of years ago. And the geological changes that are taking place before our very eyes but so imperceptibly that we cannot observe them – will continue for millions of years to come. Our role, as visitors to the magnificent national parks of the USA, in all their diverse majesty, is that of the humble outsider. With the right attitudes, we can observe, we can learn, we can participate in the natural environment, more than we ever think we can. We can, indeed, re-create ourselves and return to our normal lives – our jobs, our schoolwork, our mundane day-to-day concerns and anxieties – refreshed and conscious of a greater splendor, a greater glory, in our land.

ACADIA
Maine

Acadia National Park preserves a little of the justly celebrated Maine shoreline for the nation – preserves it undeveloped, subject only to the relentless force of the sea and the elements. The ocean crashes in remorselessly – slowly undercutting the cliffs, gradually building up the tiny beaches. It brings fogs, too – fogs that can descend suddenly and without warning, blanketing the landscape, muffling all noise, so that the familiar becomes strange and alien.

The land itself has been shaped by ice – by huge glaciers that only 70,000 years ago covered the area. Ice scooped out the lakes on Mount Desert Island. Somes Sound, which nearly bisects the island, is a glacial lake drowned as the ice melted and the sea rose. Ice rounded the mountain tops and left behind huge boulders, stranded as the ice retreated.

The park has three parts: the southern tip of Schoodic Peninsula, including Little Mosse Island; Mount Desert Island; and, some distance to the southwest, Isle au Haut. Mount Desert was named by the French navigator Samuel de Champlain, who ran aground there in 1604 as he was exploring the New England coast. Isle au Haut was named by him, too. For years the area was under French influence; the English only settled there after 1760. Shipbuilding and fishing were long the major occupations here, and commercial fishing remains important – especially for lobsters, sardines, scallops and crabs, and further offshore, cod. Today, tourism is a major business.

However, within the park the priority remains the natural world: the forest and mountains behind the sea, sea birds and seals; the sea itself, with starfish and sea urchins; and the fascinating world of the seashore, its tide-pools washed twice daily by the tides and brimming with marine life.

ARCHES
Utah

The very names arouse the visitor's anticipation: Upper Fiery Furnace, Devil's Garden, Parade of the Elephants, Garden of Eden, North Window. Contorted into strange and elaborate shapes, these huge rock formations stretch across the Utah red-rock country, north of the old pioneer Mormon settlement of Moab. Here, in a hostile and unyielding land, there are nearly a hundred towers, spires, pinnacles, windows, arches, passageways, coves, and rocks balanced one on the other, all formed by the passage of time and the unceasing impact of the elements.

The geological process began some 150 million years ago. The wind deposited a 300-foot layer of sand, now known as the Entrada Sandstone. Buried by further deposits, the Entrada Sandstone gradually hardened into rock. Later, exposed once more as the result of erosion, a lengthy process of weathering began – and still continues today. Cracks in the sandstone grew larger, forming narrow canyons. Loose sand was swept away by wind and water. The softer stone in many of the narrow walls, or fins, separating the canyons, wore away more rapidly, producing the perforations, needles and delicate silhouettes the visitor sees today.

This is a secret, at first sight deserted, land where the human visitor feels dwarfed by nature's remote and lonely grandeur. But there is some wildlife. At night, deer, coyote and foxes may appear; and in the day there are rodents, small reptiles, rabbits and birds. The sparse vegetation is chiefly piñon and juniper, but in early summer the moist places can be carpeted with a profusion of wild flowers.

BADLANDS
South Dakota

It was with good reason that the indigenous Indians called this area *mako sica* (bad land). The French-Canadian trappers who crossed the region in the early 19th century, some of the first white men ever seen here, reported in similar fashion. *Les mauvaises terres à traverser* (bad lands to cross), was their description. And something of the same atmosphere strikes the contemporary visitor. There is an eerie, hot stillness here, seemingly lifeless, almost as if one were on the moon. Bad lands, indeed.

But it was not always so. Twenty-five to thirty million years ago there was teeming animal life here. Camels and three-toed horses (both no bigger than medium-sized dogs); sabre-toothed cats; titanotheres (rhinoceros-like creatures) and tiny oreodonets – all roamed a wide, swampy plain fed by rivers from the hills to the north. Their skeletons vanished into the ooze, or were buried by sediment – and are visible now in the countless thousands of fossils that dot this area. On the fossil trail many are preserved under plexiglass on the exact spot where they were discovered.

The intervening millennia brought much geological activity. First, layers of volcanic ash from the west were deposited; visible still as the whitish sand that covers the Badlands. Gradually the rain ceased and dry winds came from the north; the mammals died, and prairie grasslands replaced the marshes. Rivers continued to flow – but now they cut into the soft land, creating spectacular shapes. Animal life has returned – prairie dogs, coyote, badger, bison, porcupine, chipmunks, snakes, jack rabbits, cottontails and pronghorn. The bison are a reminder that change is not wrought by nature alone. As recently as the early-19th century, there were huge herds of bison in this prairie country. In 1839, one such herd was estimated to cover no less than 1,350 square miles. You did not – you could not – count individual bison. You measured the herd instead. For the Plains Indians the bison were essential to life – providers of meat, clothing, shelter and tools. But the bison were doomed. The frontier was pushing rapidly westward. For the settlers, anxious to have a stake in economic prosperity, these animals were an unprofitable encumbrance. The land was needed for crops. The bison were exterminated, and by 1889 scarcely a thousand survived. Now the patient work of the National Park Service has brought them back to their natural habitat.

BIG BEND
Texas
For a little more than two-thirds of its course, from the San Juan mountains of Colorado to the Gulf of Mexico, the mighty Rio Grande forms the border between the United States and Mexico. From El Paso, the threefold junction of Mexico and the states of Texas and New Mexico, the river flows southeast to the Big Bend. Here, amid the sheer walls of a series of grand and rugged canyons, it turns abruptly northeast, before slowly falling toward the ocean again.

It is around this Big Bend that one of the nation's most majestic National Parks is situated. The land is desert, part of the Chihuahuan Desert that covers much of northern Mexico and southern Texas. Its arid soil bears cacti and a surprising variety of scrub-like vegetation: in spring, from February through May, the desert does indeed bloom. And from the desert rise up the Chisos Mountains, tall and gaunt (7,835 feet at Emory Peak, the highest in the range), and almost ghostly. The word *Chisos* is said to signify "ghost" or "spirit."

And it is down through the rocky heights of the Chisos that the Rio Grande has carved its way, during countless centuries. In its canyons – the Santa Elena, the Mariscal and the Boquillas – man is dwarfed by towering slabs of rock and can have but one sensation – that of submissive awe.

The canyons are best visited by boat. But skill and experience are required to handle a craft in tricky waters, especially in spring when they become full floods. For those not absolutely confident, the land-trails that lead into Santa Elena and Boquillas Canyons are preferable. Elsewhere in the park there are ample opportunities for hiking and horseback-riding, and for identifying the abundant plants and wildlife.

BISCAYNE
Florida
When Hurricane Andrew cut a swath across southern Florida in August, 1992, nearly everything more than three feet tall, both living and man-made, was leveled in Everglades National Park. Though also severely damaged, nearby Biscayne National Park, at exactly the spot where the storm moved onshore, was less affected because ninety-five percent of it is under water.

Because it is best enjoyed by boat or with snorkeling and scuba gear, when the 175,000-acre aquatic preserve was established in 1980 the Park Service noted, in a classic understatement, that it was "not like the other parks" it administers. But the underlying reason for its creation is a familiar one. As the cities of Miami and Miami Beach were sprawling outward, developers began lusting after the mangrove swamps lining the shores of Biscayne Bay to the south, and concerned Floridians started working to set aside the area for preservation. Their efforts led to the creation of a national monument in 1968, and eventually to its designation as Florida's second national park.

The mangrove thickets along the shore are not only breeding grounds for fish, but provide a dense barrier against erosion and, terrible as the devastation of Hurricane Andrew was, it is too awful to think of what it might have been if the developers had won their battle and Biscayne National Park had never been established. But the real treasure that was saved is the clear blue waters of Biscayne Bay itself, an environment that supports gorgeous tropical fish and underwater plants. The park extends beyond the bay into the Atlantic Ocean, where the Continental Shelf supports the growth of coral reefs, which over thousands of years have created the Florida Keys, curving 150 miles to the south. The reefs are a virtual undersea city, filled with colorful marine life whose coral homes are themselves fantastically beautiful.

Elliot Key, the wild untamed site of the park's visitor center, is the only portion of Biscayne National Park that shows any sign of development, if development is the proper word for its almost primitive facilities. Apart from the visitor center and a campground, the key and the surrounding waters haven't changed since a French naturalist visited there a century ago and noted that, "In variety, in brilliance of color, in elegance of movement, the fishes may well compare with the most beautiful assemblage of birds in tropical climates."

BRYCE CANYON
Utah
Set water to work on the land – water in the form of streams and rain, snow and ice – for millions of years, and the results can be spectacular. Bryce Canyon is evidence of this. Hundreds of tiny streams slowly cut down into the land, creating a series of

overlapping semicircular bowls, or amphitheaters. Where there were faults and fissures, the water exploited them, leaving huge slabs of rockface exposed. Water worked on these too, dissolving and cutting away the softer rock, forming gullies and creating the weird and magnificent shapes and formations – spires, needles, towers, arches – we see today.

The Pink Cliffs from which Bryce Canyon is formed are relatively young: no more than 50 to 60 million years old. They are the most youthful part of a geological "Grand Staircase," a sequence of cliffs stretching south to the northern rim of the Grand Canyon and dating back more than 225 million years.

The Pink Cliffs are well named. For here, it is not only the shapes of the rocks that fascinate and enthrall, but their colors as well. Iron oxides, manganese and copper in varying combinations create the multitude of different shades: the more manganese, the more lavender and green; the more iron, the more pink and red.

For the visitor, Bryce Canyon National Park is doubly attractive. There is spectacle, certainly, in the cliffs themselves. And there are the subtler, but no less genuine pleasures of the forest and meadows, and their extensive wildlife: well over 160 species of birds, coyote, badger, and many other night hunters, as well as mule deer, porcupine and even a few cougar, elk and black bear.

And the name Bryce? It recalls Ebenezer Bryce, a Mormon settler of Scottish descent who tried to scratch a living here from the land. His only surviving comment on his home for five years is: "A hell of a place to lose a cow!" The Paiute Indians were more lyrical, and just as accurate. Translated, their name reads: "Red rocks standing like men in a bowl-shaped canyon."

CANYONLANDS
Utah

Two rivers – the Colorado and its tributary, the Green – lie at the heart of the Canyonlands National Park. Over millions of years their force – individual at first, from the northwest and northeast, and then collective after they meet – has carved out over 100 miles of canyons, many half a mile deep. Of these, Cataract Canyon is perhaps the best known and most dramatic. For many visitors, the highlight of their vacation is an organized float trip down the Green or the Colorado and then through the Canyon. But this is just one of many hundreds of rock formations brought about by the unremitting action of water: by the rivers themselves, or by underground water eroding the 3,000-foot thick layers of salt that lie underground, causing sandstone to subside slowly into the space once filled by salt and forming long, narrow canyons, called grabens. Erosion works at varying speeds, softer rocks being attacked more easily and quickly than harder ones. The consequence is a fantastic collection of shapes that no human sculptor could imitate.

This is a desert land, with much wildlife. But for man, it is an untamed and relatively unexplored country. There is some evidence of past settlement, however. The Anasazi lived here for some thousand years, hunting and farming, making pottery and baskets. Their pictographs and petroglyphs, left on rock walls throughout Canyonlands, provide some record of their existence.

CAPITOL REEF
Utah

This national park takes its name from a reef, a ridge of rock that acts as a barrier, said to resemble the Capitol – the domed building in Washington, D.C. But the park's principal and most fascinating feature is the Waterpocket Fold: a dramatic and geologically unique fold of rock more than 100 miles long. The name came about because of the pools of water that collect in the rock after rainstorms, attracting creatures such as shrimps and spacefoot toad tadpoles.

The Fold forms the southern part of the park; a remote, spectacular area where visitors can hike in undisturbed solitude. The single road is normally passable by car, but care is needed. The fertile valley of the Fremont River lies at the center, and to the north is the confusingly named South Desert, another isolated region crossed only by creeks and dirt roads that deteriorate rapidly in flash floods. Here, too, hiking and horseback-riding are the best means of travel. Everywhere there are grand rock formations: arches, towers, pinnacles, canyons, monoliths.

Past inhabitants settled, naturally enough, along the banks of the river, and the first of these, to our knowledge, were the Fremont Indians around A.D 800. Their stone tools have been found, and the moki huts (storage bins) they built of wood and rock to preserve corn, beans and other crops, can still be seen. The Fremont left about 1200 – why is uncertain, but a severe drought may have been the reason – and until about 1880 there was no permanent settlement, although Paiute Indians did hunt there. Then the Mormons sowed crops, planted orchards (the name of their settlement was Fruita) and established a few limekilns. There was even some uranium-mining. But the land could not support a thriving community, and by the late 1960s the last inhabitants were leaving. The land was designated a national park in 1971, a move which brought it new purpose.

CARLSBAD CAVERNS
New Mexico

By rights, this should be two national parks, not one. Above ground, in the Guadalupe Mountains, there is fine, rugged hiking country, with dramatic canyons, high ridges and a magnificent abundance of wildlife: more than 600 species of plants, over 200 different kinds of birds, and many mammals, including raccoon, gopher, skunk, mule deer, bobcat, mountain lion and elk.

But it is below ground that the real wonders are to be found. The descent into the earth takes the visitor more than 800 feet into a series of majestic, awe-inspiring and immense caves: no less than 67 of them, the largest almost one mile long and 350 feet high. This is a geological wonder of the world: spectacular rock formations, iridescent stalagmites and stalactites etched with vivid colors and twisted into every imaginable shape. Devil's Spring, American Eagle, Frozen Waterfall, Frustrated Lovers, Queen's Chamber and Queen's Draperies, Hall of the Giants, Temple of the Sun – the very names suggest their grandeur.

It is simple rainwater that has created these galleries – rainwater trickling slowly down during hundreds of millions of years, imperceptibly (so imperceptibly that not even the longest-lived person would notice any change) dissolving the limestone rock.

And then there are the bats. Hundreds of thousands of bats live here – nobody knows the exact number; there are simply too many to count. From late spring to early fall, every evening at sunset, they stream out of the cavern entrance in a vast moving column that from far-off appears like a huge plume of smoke. Five thousand are said to leave every minute in search of their insect food and the exodus can take several hours. At sunrise they return ready to sleep the day through.

CHANNEL ISLANDS
California

The Channel Islands are a scattered group of eight islands off the southern coast of California. Of the eight, three – Anacapa, Santa Barbara and San Miguel – are open to visitors; another two, Santa Cruz and Santa Rosa, while still remaining in private ownership, fall, nevertheless, within the boundaries of the national park.

Reaching the islands can be tricky. The surrounding sea is frequently rough; both the ocean and the wind can rise rapidly, and fog can descend swiftly and without warning. Visitors arriving in their own boats need adequate gear and the appropriate maritime charts, plus a good deal of sailing experience. But commercial boat trips are also available.

Once safely anchored, however, you find yourself in a whole new world – a timeless one into which the technology and the priorities of mainland life cannot intrude. There are all the activities you would expect: fishing, swimming, scuba diving, hiking, camping. But even these will pale beside the majesty of an island sunset, watching a pack of sea lions swimming lazily through the water just offshore, hearing the gentle lap of tiny waves breaking on the rocks or observing a solitary seagull circle in an azure-blue sky. On all three islands there is the grotesque-looking tree sunflower, or giant coreopsis, which grows up to 10 feet high is some protected spots, as well as a wealth of other vegetation. There are fascinating tidepools to explore, where the marine life is successively submerged in water and exposed to the air in a twice-daily cycle. There are birds to spot – black oystercatchers, cormorants, guillemots, auklets, snowy plovers and many more, including brown pelicans, whose only large west-coast nesting site is on Anacapa. And then there are the sea mammals: several species of seal and sea lion are resident; and between January and March, migrating groups of gray whale pass near Anacapa.

CRATER LAKE
Oregon

Misnomer though it is, the name Crater Lake nevertheless tells you exactly what to expect: a lake lying not in a volcanic crater, for a crater may yet erupt, but in a huge caldera, or bowl created by the collapse and death of a volcano.

The collapse happened circa 5,000 B.C. – in geological time the equivalent of yesterday. For half a million years the massive 12,000-foot Mount Mazama had erupted periodically, throwing out magma from its core. Eventually the cone became so weak internally that the magma chamber emptied, and the mountain literally vanished, scattering ash over more than 5,000 square miles in an explosion whose force was more than forty-two times greater than those at Mount St. Helens in 1980. Where there had been a mountain peak there was now a large, empty, burning hot caldera. Volcanic activity continued for some time, sealing the caldera and throwing up Wizard Island, a symmetrical cinder cone.

Eventually, once the caldera had cooled sufficiently, water began to collect, deepening and widening the lake. Today, its depth (at a maximum of 1,932 feet the deepest in the USA and the sixth deepest in the world) varies by no more than three feet a year, evaporation and seepage almost exactly balancing the contribution of rain, snow and springs. Crater Lake is a closed ecological system, since no stream runs in or out, and the three fish species found there have all been introduced by man.

What its name cannot warn the visitor to expect is the sheer beauty of Crater Lake. The lake itself is a deep and vivid blue, offset in winter by the snow that lies thick all around (on the highest peaks it remains from October to July). Surrounding the lake are the rolling mountains, volcanic peaks and evergreen forests of the Cascades range – a truly spectacular setting for a truly spectacular work of nature.

DENALI
Alaska

Denali – The High One – is the apt and simple name the Indians of Alaska gave this towering, 20,320-foot giant, its twin peaks rising high and straight. Mount McKinley, the American name for the mountain, and the name by which the national park, of which it is the dramatic centerpiece, was known from its establishment in 1917 until 1980, was bestowed by a gold prospector, William A. Dickey. His reason – no doubt appropriate then, but almost laughably inappropriate now – was that William McKinley, of whose nomination for president Dickey heard on his return from the wilderness, was a fellow-supporter of the gold standard.

Within this immense and lonely wilderness man has no place. Even the hardiest and most persistent hikers must consider themselves but brief visitors, poised on the edge of an unwelcoming world. But while man cannot adapt, there is plentiful bird and animal life – no less than 37 mammal and 155 bird species. There are caribou, moving in herds of several thousand along ancient migration routes; moose; Dall sheep, which migrate in summer, too, to the high mountain crags; reindeer; elk; bison; bear and wolves. There are beaver, red squirrels, singing voles, snowshoe hares and, among the birds, golden eagles, arctic tern and warbler, golden plover and ptarmigan.

In summer, the thin top layer of the subarctic tundra melts, and enough plant life grows to support the wildlife population. Beneath, there are deep beds of permafrost – land frozen for thousands of years and drier than many deserts. High up in the mountains, although below the permanent snow line, the dry tundra supports dwarf rhododendron, forget-me-nots and a wealth of other tiny plants. Lower, in the moist tundra, there is cotton grass, sedge and dwarf shrubs, including willow and birch. In the taiga, strips of land that follow the rivers, white and black spruce grow, along with paper birch, balsam, poplar and quaking aspen.

But winter at Denali is a different world. Most birds escape by migrating to more southerly and equable climes. The animal population survives the arctic temperatures by hibernating (ground squirrel), sleeping (grizzly bear), or subsisting on concealed food stocks (beaver, red squirrel). A few of the animals, such as snowshoe hare and ptarmigan, take on a white coat and struggle to survive in a hostile environment.

EVERGLADES
Florida

The word Everglades means a marshy land covered with tall grasses – a "river of grass." And a river of grass exactly describes this unique place, the largest remaining subtropical wilderness in the USA. The entire area (less than half the Everglades itself falls within the boundaries of the national park) is a shallow, slightly tilted bowl, lined with limestone and edged with a limestone rim. Through this bowl the freshwater of Lake Okeechobee, to the north of Everglades, moves gradually, virtually imperceptibly, toward the ocean. Over thousands of years this river of grass – six inches deep and 50 miles across – has developed and maintained its own ecosystem, containing a rare blend of tropical and temperate species.

Everglades National Park was established in 1934 to preserve and protect this unique environment. Much damage had, however, already been done. The outlying areas had been built over. Hunters had virtually wiped out many species: herons and snowy and great egrets, for instance, had been pursued almost to extinction for their plumage. Land had been drained for agricultural use, and the drainage channels had both brought poisonous salt water in, killing many plants, and had dried many areas out, leaving them vulnerable to fire.

The park still faces problems, chiefly competing demands for scarce water supplies, and its ecosystem remains delicately balanced. But, for the moment, Everglades National Park is a precious sanctuary for many endangered species. Here you may see alligators and, on the saltwater rim, crocodiles; the manatee or sea cow; the cougar or Florida panther; great white herons and southern bald eagles; green sea turtle; peregrine falcon. These, and many other species, find respite here from man's continuing depredations.

The characteristic Everglades view is of a green and brown expanse of saw grass, a tooth-edged sedge that grows nearly ten feet high. The view is broken by hammocks, islands of trees and jungle poised on outcrops of limestone a few feet above the surrounding marsh. Here there are tangled thickets of palms, gumbo limbo and mahogany trees, ferns and orchids, all growing tightly together. On the coast itself, there are mangrove wildernesses and stretches of coastal prairie, where cactus, agave and yucca plants grow.

GATES OF THE ARCTIC
Alaska

When Robert Marshall first explored the central Brooks Range in 1929, he called the two peaks, Boreal Mountain, 6,666-feet high, and Frigid Crags, whose elevation is 5,550-feet, the "Gates of the Arctic." The peaks stand guard over the north fork of the Koyukuk River, one hundred miles north of the Arctic Circle.

Thanks to Marshall's descriptions and the enthusiasm of others who followed him, more than eight million acres in North-central Alaska along the Arctic Divide has become a national park,

preserving one of the very best large wildernesses in the entire world. Wilderness is the key word at Gates of The Arctic National Park; it is hardly the kind of place one would go for a Sunday afternoon picnic and a walk in the woods. The Brooks Range, the northernmost extension of the Rocky Mountains, is a rugged one, but although its peaks soar as high as 8,510-feet at Mt. Igikpak, it isn't as intimidating as some other mountains in Alaska, nor in some parts of the lower forty-eight states, either. There are glaciers on its slopes, but smaller than many in the Last Frontier because the region is relatively dry. Not much snow falls, but not much of it melts, either. But for all that, Gates of the Arctic is a land of clear, clean rivers, six of which are well respected by white water enthusiasts, and of deep, blue alpine lakes. North of the Arctic Divide, the park is treeless, alpine tundra; but the lower valleys on the south side support forests of willow, white spruce and aspen. In the northern reaches of the park the taiga supports sparse stands of black spruce.

All the vegetation in the park grows quite slowly, so there is less density of wildlife. But it is home to grizzly bears, black bears, caribou, moose and other species, as well as hawks, owls, ptarmigan and a varied population of migrating birds that usually arrive during the spring breakup, which begins in April, although many streams are still clogged with ice in June, when the sun shines twenty-four hours a day. There is a human population in the park, too, most notably in the Inuit village at Anaktuvuk Pass. The village is served by a scheduled airline, but most visitors to the Gates of the Arctic rely on air taxis. There are no roads, except the unpaved Dalton Highway crossing the mountains toward the oil-rich North Slope through the Trans-Alaska Pipeline corridor.

GLACIER
Montana

The Waterton/Glacier International Peace Park is a unique national park, a symbol of co-operation and understanding between the nations. That the two nations concerned – the USA and Canada – are old and staunch friends and allies, is less important than the symbolism of the decision made in 1932 by the Canadian Parliament and the US Congress to merge their respective national parks. It was a recognition that the natural landscape and the creatures and vegetation that inhabit it are world assets, not purely national ones. The lesson, over a half century later, still needs to be recalled.

And what a landscape it is, with hundreds of miles of towering, snowcapped peaks, spectacular canyons, rushing waterfalls, ice-blue lakes and deep green forests. This is glacier country. No less than four times in the last three million years, thick sheets of ice have covered it, sculpting the land as we see it today, creating peaks and passes, ridges and valleys. But before that – at least sixty million years before, perhaps more – the land itself had been shaped in a massive series of upheavals. Ancient rocks, originally on the ocean floor, thrust themselves up, and a huge slab of rock was propelled about 50 miles eastward over the existing, and much younger, mountain range.

There are three distinct climates here. On the western side of the park the climate is Pacific – warm and moist, with fir, pine, spruce and larch forests. In the east, prairie conditions prevail, with red and white geraniums, asters, Indian paintbrush and other characteristic flora. In the Alpine areas, the wild flowers are at their most magnificent – gentian, glacier lily, heather. And here, too, there is a wide variety of wildlife, often easily visible from the many hundreds of miles of trail in the back country: bighorn sheep, black bear, mountain goat, moose, wapiti.

GLACIER BAY
Alaska

One of America's most popular vacation options is a cruise up the Inside Passage of the Alaska Panhandle. Though every nautical mile of the trip is fascinating, most cruise ship passengers agree that the best part is the side trip into Glacier Bay. The first to cruise along that route was the British explorer George Vancouver, who sailed past the bay in 1794, but never noted it on his charts because the strait leading into it was choked with ice, and he never knew of the wonders that lay beyond. The ice has retreated in the years since, not only giving access into Glacier Bay, but allowing scientists a rare opportunity to study how plant and animal life was reestablished after the last great glaciers retreated from southern Canada and the northern United States. John Muir described it best when he explored the area in 1879 and said it is " ... original nature, a landscape like a thought not yet formed."

There are sixteen glaciers meeting the waters of Glacier and Taylor Bays in the 3,280,000-acre park, twelve of which routinely "calve" huge icebergs into the water. There are also dozens more, some retreating, some advancing and some that seem to be going nowhere at all, within the park's boundaries in the surrounding St. Elias Mountains. And if the rivers of ice provide spectacular scenery, the mountains themselves give them plenty of competition. The highest peak, Mount Fairweather, is 15,300-feet high, and although there are eighteen higher mountains in North America (half of them in Alaska), Fairweather is only fifteen miles away from the park's lowest point at sea level. Glacier Bay is also a landscape of spectacular ice-carved fjords and a back country wilderness that supports a large population of grizzly and black bears, including a rare color phase of the black bear, at which time its fur is blue. The animal population also includes moose, wolves, blacktail deer, mountain goats and bald eagles. In addition to its huge population of marine birds, the park is also a major stopping place for birds using the Pacific flyway in the spring and fall. The waters of the bay are rich in plankton, the staff of life for humpback and killer whales as well as for porpoises, sea lions and seals who consider Glacier Bay heaven on earth. They are probably right.

GRAND CANYON
Arizona

Words genuinely fail: the language is too poor in adjectives to do justice to the wonder of the Grand Canyon. Even the plain statistics – 277 miles long measured along the river, between 600 feet and 18 miles wide, and about a mile deep – cannot truly convey the atmosphere of this most celebrated and most impressive of all the United States' many natural beauties. The photographs help. From them the reader can begin to appreciate the Grand Canyon's stunning grandeur; its ever-changing light and colors. But it is perhaps only on an extended visit, when there is time to observe and explore, that one can see into the Canyon's heart, and come to terms a little with this amazing work of nature.

It is the river that has created this spectacle; the swift-flowing Colorado that some 25 million years ago began to scour the flat plateau, cutting through layer after layer of rock. The scouring continues, as it has done for eons, at the rate of about six-and-a-half inches every thousand years. This entire area is ancient: the first rocks were formed some 1,700 million years ago, when mountains were thrust up, only to be almost entirely eroded again. The rocks of these first mountains can be seen at the foot of the Inner Gorge, where the Colorado now runs. Another upheaval produced more mountains, and these again were almost entirely eroded. Rocks from this era form the second layer of basement rocks in the gorge. Some 550 million years ago the canyon area became a basin, collecting over the next 300 million years layers of sandstone, shale and limestone that form the upper parts of the canyon walls. Finally, only 65 million years ago, the earth's crust started to rise; snow and rain from the Rockies began to search for a way to the sea, and the Colorado River started to establish its course.

The descent into the Canyon is thus a journey into our geological past, each of the multicolored layers representing a different era, down to some of the oldest rocks known on earth. It is also a journey through numerous climatic zones: in fact the Canyon has six of the northern hemisphere's seven life zones. This has fascinating consequences for the animal life of the area. The north and south rims of the Canyon may not be many miles apart, but for many species the gap is unbridgeable: to cross it would mean passing through life zones with unsuitable climate and food. Thus, the Abert and Kaibab squirrels. Their habits are very similar, and before the Canyon was formed they surely had a common ancestor. But now the Abert lives south of the Canyon, the Kaibab in the north, each remaining isolated from the other.

GRAND TETON
Wyoming

Like so much else on this continent of stunning natural beauty, the Grand Teton range was formed as a result of cataclysmic geological upheaval. In common with the Sierra Nevada, the Grand Tetons are fault-block mountains: a steep escarpment rising sheer out of the plain on the eastern side, with gently sloping foothills to the west. What happened, many millions of years ago, was that pressures in the earth's crust transformed what had been the seabed into mountains. Still greater pressures made the rocks break into two parts along a fault. The western half was tilted up and over the eastern half, creating the western foothills and the steep eastern face. The newly uplifted mountains forced the clouds from over the Pacific to rise higher, increasing rainfall on the west side of the mountains. The streams swelled, and those flowing east, which now had less distance to go, carved out deeper canyons, carrying debris onto the plain. Glaciers continued the process, deepening the canyons and scouring out glacial lakes.

These, then, are the geological events. The result is a spectacular mountain range. The three stars in a firmament of majesty are the three highest peaks, named *Les Trois Tetons* by an early French traveler: Grand, Middle and South; 13,770, 12,798 and 12,505 feet high respectively. Accompanying them are deep-green forests, brilliant glaciers, steep canyons, ice-blue lakes and streams. Here elk, moose, black and grizzly bear, bighorn sheep, beaver, weasel, coyote and many other animals dwell undisturbed.

One natural curiosity deserves mention. The Continental Divide – the watershed between east and west – runs through Grand Tetons National Park. Water falling on one side eventually reaches the Atlantic, while on the other side it makes its way to the Pacific. High in the Tetons lies Two Ocean Pass, a tiny lake with two outlets. One, Atlantic Creek, pursues its course to the Gulf of Mexico, which feeds into the Atlantic Ocean, via the Missouri and the Mississippi rivers; while the other, Pacific Creek, flows to the Pacific by way of the Columbia River.

GREAT BASIN
Nevada
The wide basins and high mountains of the Snake Range on the eastern edge of Nevada, a few miles from the Utah border, became a national park in 1986. Before then, a square-mile section of the eastern slope of the 13,603-foot Wheeler Peak had been the Lehman Caves National Monument surrounding the beautiful limestone caves discovered by homesteader Absalom Lehman in 1885. The caverns, in which no two rooms are alike, are filled with unusual formations, some that look like carved faces, some that describe the shapes of animals, some that take the imagination on flights of unearthly fantasy. In some places the stone looks like rippling waterfalls, and everywhere the ceilings are adorned with fantastic, multicolored patterns. The floors are strewn with saucer-like little terraces made by calcified water, and the walls and ceilings are decorated with crystals in hundreds of frosty shapes. Some of the stalactites are ribbonlike and translucent, making them deserving of the term "bacon strips." Others have formed into stone structures called "tom-toms" because of the resounding booming sound that is made when they are struck.

Outdoors, the 76,800-acre park, in addition to the craggy mountain peaks, includes such wonders as the seventy-five-foot limestone Lexington Arch. Wheeler Peak has a rare forest of bristlecone pines, which are among the oldest living things on earth, with specimens proven to be more than 10,000 years old. The park also includes forests of pine, spruce, fir and mountain mahogany, and its aspen-lined streams and creeks are filled with trout. There are mule deer in the high meadows and cougar are sometimes spotted in the back country. The skeletal remains of prehistoric Indians have been found in the area, and grazing cattle are a living reminder of the ranchers who still make their living from the land surrounding the park.

GREAT SMOKY MOUNTAINS
North Carolina, Tennessee
The statistics concerning this national park are quite simply fantastic. Within its half million acres there are over 1,400 different kinds of flowering plants; 350 species of mosses and related plants; about 2,000 species of fungi and some 130 kinds of tree. The tulip trees reach nearly 200 feet into the air, chestnut

oaks 100 feet. Nearly 250 bird species have been seen in the mountains, and some 50 mammal, 40 reptile and 70 fish species dwell here. Three quarters of the park is wilderness: there are 700 miles of streams, 800 of trails and sixteen peaks over 6,000 feet – the tallest, Clingmans Dome, is 6,643 feet high. The land itself is old – 400 million years old, which is three times as ancient as the Rocky Mountains.

But probably the most remarkable fact about the park is not another item in a long list of statistics. It is the very fact of the area's survival. For thousands of years after man first walked the earth, the Great Smoky Mountains lay undisturbed, barely marked by human intervention. The change came in the early 19th century, when European settlers arrived. The forests vanished, as did the indigenous Cherokees, and agriculture, logging and mining all but ruined the land forever.

That this seems barely credible now is a tribute to the successful conservation policies practiced in the park over the last half-century. Some 40 per cent of the original forest – the forest that the Cherokees knew – remains: a moist, misty and deeply wooded world of coves, waterfalls, tumbling streams and balds, that might never have been threatened. Balds are an interesting phenomenon of the Great Smoky Mountains. There is no treeline in the park, and the highest peaks are thickly wooded. Balds are smaller peaks, yet treeless and with a cover of grass and sedge, or heaths such as rhododendron or laurel.

Some eight million visitors come here each year. The park absorbs them all, offering each individual the opportunity for real physical and mental recreation.

GUADALUPE MOUNTAINS
Texas
A barrier reef in Texas, much like the celebrated reef off the coast of Queensland, Australia, seems a paradox. But such a reef is at the heart of the Guadalupe Mountains National Park. About 280 to 225 million years ago a large, shallow, salty inland sea covered some 10,000 square miles of what is now Texas and New Mexico. A reef was built up of lime-secreting algae and other organisms and a lagoon formed between the reef and the land. The lagoon was gradually filled in, and the reef was buried. For the most part it has remained that way, deep beneath the hot, lifeless Texas plain. But in a few spots it is exposed, most notably on the eastern escarpment of the Guadalupe mountains, in Carlsbad Caverns National Park and, on the Texas side of the state line, in Guadalupe Mountains National Park.

For the geologically-minded visitor, the spot to head for is McKittrick Canyon, in whose 1,900-foot north wall there is a remarkable cross-section that includes the core of the reef itself, plus fore-reef and back-reef deposits.

This single feature, a reminder of a Texan landscape very different from the present one, should not lead us to ignore the many other diverse environmental features of this national park. There are no less than four separate climatic zones, varying between those prevailing in southern Canada and in northern Mexico; and three ecological zones, between the lowest point in the park, 3,650 feet above sea level, and the tip of Guadalupe Peak, 8,749 feet up. There is both desert and high-country vegetation; a rarely-found association. The abundant wildlife –

more than 200 species of bird, and 52 species of reptiles and amphibians have been recorded – is likewise unusually mixed. This is the northernmost limit for many Mexican species, and the southern and easternmost for many species from the Rocky Mountains.

HALEAKALA
Hawaii

Two quite distinct areas make up this national park on the Hawaiian island of Maui. There is the crater of Mount Haleakala which has given its name to the park – a strikingly-bizarre landscape that seems to belong to the moon rather than to our own planet. And, in startling contrast, there is Kipahulu – a region of pools, cascades and waterfalls, pastoral valleys and grasslands, rain forests and rugged coastal cliffs.

Like all the Hawaiian islands, Maui is the product of millions of years of undersea volcanic eruptions. Originally there were two separate volcanoes, whose summits slowly climbed from the seabed and eventually emerged above the waves. The island was formed when they were joined by an isthmus created by lava, alluvium and ash. Haleakala is the larger of these volcanoes (it stands some 12,000 feet above sea level and about 30,000 feet above the ocean floor). The crater is, in fact, misnamed. It is the result, not of volcanic activity, but of prolonged erosion during a time, many millions of years ago, when the volcano was dormant. Since then, however, multicolored symmetrical cones up to 600 feet high have been formed from ash, cinders and spatter blown out of vents within the crater.

Now, Haleakala (the name means House of the Sun) is quiet once more. There were two minor lava flows at a low level in 1790, and earthquake records show that all is not yet settled deep within the mountain. But it is now almost certain that it will never erupt again.

On its eastern edge, the park gives protection to the fragile ecosystem of the Kipahulu area. Native birds survive here still (in many other parts of the island chain, species imported by white settlers have virtually obliterated the native species), as does a large tract of the koa and 'ohi'a rain forest, still almost undisturbed by civilization. Here, too, there are bamboo, mango, guava and kukui, and the 'Ohe'o stream, normally placid, occasionally torrential, joining the numerous sparkling pools.

HAWAII VOLCANOES
Hawaii

The Hawaiian Islands are simply a chain of volcanic mountains. Over many millions of years molten rock, or magma, has forced its way from deep in the earth up through the ocean bed. The magma slowly forms enormous undersea mountains, mountains so large that some eventually emerge through the waves as islands. Many of the volcanoes thus formed are now extinct: the turmoil way beneath their summits is stilled, and the lava no longer flows. The reason is because the island chain is moving – slowly, almost imperceptibly – some two to three inches a year northwest, but moving nevertheless. The Hawaiian Islands are positioned on a section of the earth's crust known as the Pacific Plate, and it is this plate that is on the move, cutting the volcanoes off from their source of magma.

Of all the Hawaiian Islands, Hawaii itself is the largest. Its three greatest volcanoes are Mauna Kea, Mauna Loa and Kilauea, and the last two of these make the centerpiece – the stars indeed – of the Hawaii Volcanoes National Park. And great they are: Mauna Kea and Mauna Loa are claimed to be the greatest mountain masses on the planet, measured from the ocean floor. Mauna Kea rises 15,000 feet before it breaks the waves, and then continues a further 13,796 feet; Mauna Loa is almost as high, and Kilauea only some 5,000 feet shorter.

Nor are these volcanoes extinct. Mauna Loa and Kilauea are among the most active anywhere on earth. Kilauea erupts almost every year, pushing lava from its summit and from rifts in its side in spectacular displays. On a number of trails that cross the park molten lava lies beneath the crater surfaces. Most spectacular of all is Mauna Ulu, or "Growing Mountain," a new parasitic lava shield on the east side of Kilauea, from which huge amounts of lava have poured.

Hawaii Volcanoes National Park is a vivid reminder that nature is not still; that geological forces remain at work.

HOT SPRINGS
Arkansas

This is a most unusual national park. Its heart is not an awesome stretch of landscape, or an outstanding environmental feature, but a far smaller and more modest manifestation of nature: a series of hot, therapeutic springs bubbling out of the ground. It is also far older as a protected resource than any other national park, having been set aside as a reservation as early as 1832, well before Europeans had even set foot in many of the areas described elsewhere in this book, and before the concept of national parks was formalized at Yellowstone in 1872. But its history long predates that. For centuries before the first white man came (the Spanish explorer Hernando de Soto in 1541), Native Americans had gathered here on neutral ground; a place to which members of any peoples could come in perfect safety. The USA acquired the springs in 1803 as part of the Louisiana Purchase from France, along with a vast stretch of territory in what are now the Southern and Western States. And almost immediately visitors were arriving to take the waters. Soon the federal government went into partnership with private interests, developing bathhouses and ensuring the water supply. In this century, the 1920s and late 1940s have been boom periods – and although numbers of visitors have declined in recent years, the resort flourishes still.

What, then, is it that attracts seekers of health and relaxation? As at other spas, it is the quality of the waters. Here the thermal water is naturally sterile: no bacteria whatsoever are present. It gushes from the ground at a constant temperature – 143 degrees Fahrenheit – and contains traces of a number of valuable minerals: calcium, magnesium, bicarbonate and fluoride among them. Steam cabinets, whirlpools, massages, alcohol rubs, hot and cold packs, and many other treatments, enable visitors to obtain full benefit and refreshment from the waters.

And these waters may be remarkably old. The water that gushes forth from the springs today, started as rainwater that was absorbed deep into the earth through fractures and cracks in the rock. Heated by contact with hot rocks, it then returned slowly to the surface, in a cycle that can take as long as 4,000 years.

ISLE ROYALE
Michigan

Isle Royale is a rare phenomenon in the late 20th century. It is a natural habitat, some would say a true wilderness – the only one in the US, outside Alaska, that remains scarcely disturbed by man. There were once trading posts here, and beaver-trappers and copper-miners came. But they have long since gone and nature has once more reasserted herself.

There is genuine isolation here. The devices of civilization hardly intrude: there is no public telephone system, for instance. The island's sense of remoteness is enhanced by its physical position in the middle of Lake Superior – 15 miles from the nearest shore, and a three to six hour boat journey away from the mainland ports. Even in the height of summer, bad weather and rough water can delay or postpone the voyage.

When you arrive, you will find a world of dense vegetation and forests, lakes, streams and offshore islands. The best way to explore is by boat or on foot. There are 160 miles of foot trails, one of the most spectacular of which runs along the Greenstone Ridge – the island's central backbone. There is fishing too, and an amazing variety of aquatic environments: streams, rivers, warm-water ponds and the waters of Lake Superior itself.

The story of two of the most interesting wildlife species on the island is fascinating. Moose reached Isle Royale by swimming there sometime early this century. By the 1930s there were so many that food stocks could not cope, and the moose began to die. A fire in 1936 made matters worse, and numbers fell sharply, only to increase yet again as fodder grew once more. But in the winter of 1948-9, a pack of wolves crossed the ice from Canada, established itself on the island, and now the two species, prey and predator, together create a natural balance: the wolves culling the weak and old moose, thus maintaining a healthy population.

KATMAI
Alaska

In 1918, the National Geographic Society sent an expedition into the Katmai Valley in Southwestern Alaska which, six years earlier, had become known locally as the Valley of Ten Thousand Smokes, after Mount Katmai and nearby Novaupta both erupted in an explosion that buried the valley under a thick coating of ash and pumice. The explorers interviewed a local Indian, known as American Pete, an eyewitness to the eruption who told them, " ... Katmai mountain blow up with lots of fire and fire come down trail with lot of smoke. Me go fast ... hell of a job! Now I go back every year ... good place, too, you bet! Lot moose, bear, deer; lot fish. No many mosquitoes." But, he added, if the Valley of Ten Thousand Smokes was a nice place to visit, "never can go back to live."

When the mountains exploded in 1912, the valley was not only changed for all time, buried under a cubic mile of ash, but the nearby island of Kodiak was covered with six feet of the stuff. Mount Katmai itself collapsed into a caldera, which is now filled with a beautiful green lake surrounded by a halo of glaciers, possibly the youngest in the world, and the only ones whose exact date of origin is known. But if the legacy of vulcanism makes Katmai a fascinating place, it is only one of the things that make this one of the crown jewels of the national park system. As American Pete noted, it is a wonderland of wildlife. It is the biggest sanctuary for grizzly bears anywhere in the world, and the huge 400 to 800-pound animals never go hungry, thanks to the profusion of salmon in the park's rivers. Although there are no trails or roads in its nearly four million acres of wilderness, the bears have created any number of paths from one fishing hole to another, a great convenience for hikers – as long as they tread carefully. Katmai's forest and tundra also support large numbers of moose, caribou, foxes, lynxes and other wildlife, including beavers who are hard at work changing the landscape. There are bald eagles everywhere in the park, too, and offshore in the Pacific sea otters play in waters that are home to seals, sea lions and whales. Many fishermen consider Katmai the ultimate experience. The rainbow trout, grayling and mackinaws are bigger, more numerous and hungrier, they say, than almost anywhere else on earth. There is plenty of competition from the bears, of course, but that only adds to the challenge.

KENAI FJORDS
Alaska

The Kenai Peninsula, stretching south from Anchorage to form the eastern border of Cook Inlet, owes its rugged beauty to centuries of action by glaciers, and most of the landscape of Kenai Fjords National Park is still dominated by glaciers radiating out from the 300-square-mile Harding Ice Field. It is one of the most scenic spots in all of Alaska, itself quite possibly the most scenic of all the fifty states. But the fjords of Kenai are also among the most treacherous waters anywhere on the continent. Fronting on the stormy Gulf of Alaska, an unpredictable body of water by any standard, they have unusually strong tidal currents and many of the poorly charted bays are laced with uncharted rocks. One reason is that this is a land still forming; the Alaskan earthquake of 1964 alone dropped as much as seven feet of the Kenai coastline into the bay. But the dramatic scenery of the park is enhanced by the harbor seals that hold court at the entrances of most of the fjords, as well as the sea lions that breed on the hundreds of offshore islands. In between, the coastal waters are havens for schools of whales and playgrounds for charming sea otters.

The peaks of the Kenai Mountains, which rise up to a plateau a mile above the sea, trap moisture-laden clouds that dump thirty-five to sixty-five feet of snow on them each year. The result is one of the biggest icepacks in the world, which has been working for centuries carving deep valleys. In the meantime, the mountains are being slowly dragged into the water by shifting tectonic plates, and what were once high valleys are now flooded, steep-sided coastal fjords whose rock walls tower above drowned alpine meadows. The western side of the Kenai Peninsula is a nearly two-million-acre wildlife refuge that was once known as the National Moose Range. Large parts of it were destroyed in forest fires, the most notable of which burned out of control in the 1940s, and then again in 1969. What might appear to have been a disaster actually encouraged a second growth of willow, birch and aspen, the favorite food of moose.

KOBUK VALLEY
Alaska

Picture a place where the summer temperature sometimes tops one hundred degrees and where shifting, crescent-shaped sand dunes stretch as far as the eye can see, and Alaska is probably the last place on earth that fits the image. But there at the foot of the western Brooks Range, the Kobuk River flows through a beautiful forested valley that includes twenty-five square miles of landscape that would be more appropriate in the Sahara than in northern Alaska, just below the Arctic Circle. The sand dunes, created during the last ice age by glaciers to the north, are much more than a curious freak of nature. The Kobuk Valley was ice-free during the era of the great glaciers and, as an Arctic steppe, its grasslands attracted the large mammals of the Pleistocene period escaping the advancing sheets of ice. The animals have long gone, of course, but many of the plants that supported them when they lived still survive, along with other subarctic plants that stabilize the dunes. The valley was also a haven for humans, and it has become one of North America's most important archaeological sites, with more than thirty layers of artifacts tracing the presence of man back some 12,500 years.

The park, which is located on the dividing line between the forests of the south and the treeless tundra of the north, has been an important migration route for Arctic caribou for centuries, and great herds of the animals fill the valley both in winter and summer. It is also a crossroads of the Asian and North American flyways used by migrating birds in the spring and fall. Permanent residents of the park include grizzly and black bears, Dall sheep and wolves, among other creatures. Unlike most national parks, Kobuk Valley also has a human population. There are several Inuit villages inside its boundaries, providing a rare glimpse into the ancient way of life of their ancestors.

LAKE CLARK
Alaska
Easily one of the most diverse regions of Alaska, the 3,655,000-acre Lake Clark National Park, 150 miles southwest of Anchorage, includes deep blue lakes, rivers frothing with white water, gentle streams, roaring waterfalls, mighty glaciers, pounding ocean surf, flower-strewn meadows and spectacular mountains, including two active volcanoes. The park contains the junction of two great mountain chains, the Aleutian and the Alaskan ranges, and its namesake, Lake Clark, is the sixth-largest inland body of water in the state. Just outside the park's boundaries, Lake Iliamna has the only population of inland seals in the country, and its watershed provides a third of all the red salmon catch in the United States. The wilderness is home to grizzly and brown bears, as well as moose, wolves and wolverines.

The park's dominant feature is the peaks of the Chigmit mountains, at the junction of the two ranges that merge here, including the steaming volcanoes, Redoubt and Iliamna, both more than 10,000-feet high. The steep slopes of the mountains plunge abruptly into Cook Inlet, where such sea birds as puffin, cormorant and kittiwake populate huge cliffside rookeries. Lake Clark is a virtually untouched wilderness with no roads and no marked trails. But it is one of the oldest sites of human habitation in Alaska, with evidence of a Native American population stretching far back into prehistory. It was also the site of early Russian trading posts, marking the first European presence in the Last Frontier, and the first Anglo-Americans in Alaska also explored the Lake Clark area.

LASSEN VOLCANIC
California
May 30, 1914: quite unexpectedly, without any warning signs, Mount Lassen breaks some two centuries of inactivity and erupts, sending a stream of molten lava downhill. The crater, on the north slope near the summit, is quite small at first, only 45 feet wide, but within two weeks it grows to 1,500 feet in diameter. Ash and steam reach a height of three miles. Almost a year of quiet follows. Then, on the night of May 19, 1915, there is another explosion, far more devastating than before. Molten lava rushes down Lost Creek and Hat Creek; the steam released with it melts the snow and a horrendous, tumultuous mud slide, at times 18 feet deep, destroys everything in its path. A few days later, yet another explosion of steam and hot ash wipes out whatever has managed to survive. The land is stripped clean, and some five million feet of timber are lost.

Mount Lassen is quiet now. Visitors can enjoy the serene beauty of the national park – the lakes (there are more than fifty); the deep green forests; the flower-filled valleys. They can follow the 150 miles of foot trails, and look for the birds and animals that make their home here.

But reminders of nature's might remain. Bumpass Hell (named for a man who fell into a mudpot in 1865 – and survived) is a seething area of hot springs, mudpots and fumaroles. The Devastated Area still remains denuded of vegetation nearly seventy years after the explosion that overwhelmed it. The Hot Rock – a huge boulder of lava – lies where it came to rest in 1915. Its name comes from the fact that it remained hot for days.

Until 1980, one could say of Lassen that it was the only volcano on the US mainland to have erupted this century. But the dramatic explosion of Mount St. Helens, 400 miles to the north, in the same volcanic range, reminds us that inside, Lassen remains in turmoil. The events of 1914 and 1915 could repeat themselves.

MAMMOTH CAVE
Kentucky
There are 150 miles of explored passageways in this subterranean complex, and many times that length remain unexplored. The names the early speleologists gave the caverns, rooms and passages are a vivid demonstration of their awe at what they found: Frozen Niagara, Grand Central Station, Rock of Gibraltar, Rocky Mountains, Old Bull's Concert Hall. It is an impressive, solitary world underground: long passages stretching and disappearing into the distance, large multicolored stalactites, weird shapes chiselled out of the rock.

This is a limestone cave. Its story started millions of years ago under the sea, when the skeletons of tiny marine animals collected and solidified to form limestone. Later, after earth movements had brought the limestone onto dry land, a slow attack by water began. Exploiting all the cracks and crevices, the water gradually seeped through – dissolving the limestone, its sediments also scouring out chambers. The final chapter was a fall in water level underground, which left us with the network of caves we enjoy today.

There is much to do above ground, too, in Mammoth Cave National Park. There are trails through the beautiful hardwood forests, some leading to springs that emerge from the caves beneath the walkers' feet. There is the forest wildlife to observe. And there is the Green River, which runs through the park, to enjoy.

MESA VERDE
Colorado

Mesa Verde means "green table," and the name must date from some time in the middle of the 18th century, when the first Spanish explorers reached the area. But, although they had been unoccupied for several hundred years, the mesas – high plateaus dotted with spruce, juniper and piñon, and cut through by deep canyons – had been the site of a flourishing and elaborate Indian civilization. The evidence, preserved for us to marvel at today, consists chiefly of groups of dwellings large enough to house an entire community, and built in caves on the cliff face. These are elaborate shelters: the Spruce Tree House, for example, has eight ceremonial chambers and no less than 114 living rooms.

Little is known of the cliff-dwellers. They seem to have moved down from the mesas into their precarious cavern dwellings toward the end of the 12th century. Why is uncertain. One reason may have been fear of attack: the open mesa was vulnerable to assault, the enclosed canyon far more secure. Whatever the reasons, they must have been good ones, for life can hardly have been congenial there: extremes of heat in summer and cold in winter, and a long climb up to the fields on the mesas. Within a century the cliff dwellers had vanished entirely, driven out, it is now thought, by prolonged droughts and bad harvests at the end of the 13th century.

Before the move to the cliffs, the mesa tops had been occupied for some six centuries, first by people known as Basket Makers, because of the elaborate examples of their skills they left behind. They lived in pithouses dug in the ground. Their successors were Pueblo Indians who dwelt first in houses made of poles, sticks and mud, and later, during the 12th century, in sturdy, sizeable, stone-built houses, some of which had as many as three stories and fifty rooms.

For us today, fascinating examples of many of these different dwellings remain, together with an enthralling collection of everyday objects, once discarded and abandoned but now preserved for our interest and enjoyment.

MOUNT RAINIER
Washington

A jagged, eternally snowcapped peak rises high in the distance and dominates the land around for many miles. Beneath it lies a dense green enclosing forest, and fields and valleys of wild flowers in gorgeous display. Small wonder then that Mount Rainier exerts such a pull, as it is for many a place of recreation.

At 14,410 feet, Mount Rainier – or Takhoma, to give it its Indian name – is not quite the highest peak in the continental US, but many claim that it is the most striking. It is, in fact, a dormant volcano, though not necessarily a dead one. On the summit there are two craters, and although there has been no major eruption for two thousand years, and no minor one since

1870, steam still rises from the craters' edges, melting the ice cap a little and creating steam caves. On occasions these have been lifesavers, when climbers trapped by bad weather have found refuge in them.

No less than twenty-seven named glaciers surround the summit – an expanse of ice covering some 35 square miles, slowly moving downhill, still shaping and reshaping the mountain. In warm weather an avalanche of ice, snow and rock may suddenly break off from a glacier and hurtle downward, or mud and rock trapped beneath the ice may work free and slide down in an unstoppable mudflow.

Below the snow line, the subalpine meadowland – home of deer, mountain goats and marmots – is vibrant and full of color. Wild flowers abound in astonishing numbers: no less than 700 different species have been counted. Each year, spring bursts into life at successively higher levels as the snow melts, and suddenly there is blossom everywhere and carpets of blooms beneath one's feet. So tightly packed are the forests further down the slopes – Pacific silver firs between 3,000 and 5,000 feet; Douglas fir, big-leaf maple, red cedars, western hemlock below 3,000 feet – that the sun can scarcely penetrate, and the valley floors are draped with moss and ferns.

NORTH CASCADES
Washington

This spectacular national park, at the northern end of the Cascades range in northern Washington State, contains some splendidly wild and isolated country. Much of the land is virtually unexplored, and is accessible only to experienced back-country hikers willing to take to the cross-country mountain trails. Those who do so find a stimulating and challenging world of glaciers and crevasses, cliffs, spires and pinnacles, snowfields, high peaks and tumbling waterfalls. There are meadows full of Alpine flowers, and forests of western red cedars and Douglas firs.

These are relatively young mountains: a volcanic range whose present shape was etched during the geologically recent ice ages, which carved their steep slopes, deep valleys and jagged ridges. Remnants of the ice ages are found in the many glaciers in the park – no less than 318, which is more than half of all the glaciers in the USA's lower 48 states. The glaciers are formed when moisture-bearing clouds, coming in from the Pacific, are forced upward on the western side of the park. Their moisture falls as snow which, since the rate of melt is lower than the snowfall, compacts into ice.

The North Cascades National Park is part of a rather larger recreation area.The park itself is split into two units, northern and southern, divided by the Ross Lake National Recreation Area. Here, there are three dams built between 1924 and 1949 on the Skagit River to provide electricity for Seattle. And at the south-eastern tip of the park lies Lake Chelan National Recreation Area, a magnificent wilderness in the Stehekin Valley. Lake Chelan, resting in a glacial trough, is among the nation's deepest lakes: its bed is 1,500 feet down, some 400 feet below sea level. Stehekin itself, an isolated community at the head of the lake, can be reached only by foot, boat or plane. But it is a trip well worth the effort.

OLYMPIC
Washington

Within the 900,000 acres of the Olympic National Park lies a fascinating variety of wilderness: rain forests, Alpine meadows, snowcapped peaks, crystal streams and rivers, and a long and rugged stretch of Pacific coastline. It is an untouched land – virtually as pure as the day when white men first came here. Settlement started in the mid 19th century, with fur trapping and timber cutting along the coast. But the interior remained unknown until 1890, when a party of five explorers set out to discover its wonders. Returning awed at what they had seen, they proposed a national park. Twenty years later their suggestion became reality, and a substantial area, later extended, came under federal protection.

It is the Pacific Ocean, crashing relentlessly onto the park's 50-mile shore, that creates the environment here. Wind and clouds gusting in from the west rise as they cross the coast and reach the mountains, shedding their water on the peaks. Mount Olympus, at 7,965 feet the grand centerpiece of the park, is the wettest place in the continental US, receiving some 200 inches of rain every year. From the peaks the water falls rapidly, often as meltwater from glaciers, becoming first a rapid stream and then a rushing river. At 1,000 feet the rain forests begin: a dense, green jungle of trees, moss, shrubs, fallen trunks and branches, in places quite impenetrable.

Above the rain forest lies a belt of temperate forest; above that, mountain and subalpine forest, and finally, over 5,000 feet, the Alpine zone is reached – a merciless tundra in which only arctic plants, mosses and lichens can survive. On the shore, of course, there is yet another, quite different, environment, with sea stacks, cliffs and tidepools.

The wildlife is as varied as the environment. Deer, marmot, black bear and Roosevelt elk (safe now from the hunter's gun) can all be seen. Along the coast there are raccoons and harbor seals, sometimes even migrating gray whales.

As an area of natural unspoiled landscape, Olympic National Park is unsurpassed. Come here to hike, climb, fish or ride. But, above all come here to learn from the natural world. You will not be disappointed.

PETRIFIED FOREST
Arizona

"Painted Desert and its trees turned to stone" was the way US Army surveyors and mappers described this area when they first crossed it in the 19th century.

The trees "turned to stone" are indeed just that. Once, perhaps some 200 million years ago, trees did grow here. Floods felled them, burying them in marshy land. Ground water containing large quantities of silica and other minerals gradually seeped through the wood, dissolving its fibers. In its place were substituted exact copies of the trees, including their rings and cells, but in minerals, not in wood. Finally, after numerous geological upheavals, erosion set to work, slowly removing the shales and sandstones – sometimes as much as 3,000 feet deep – that covered the petrified trees, leaving them exposed and scattered across the land.

These trees, some as large as 100 feet long and eight feet in diameter, bear an uncanny resemblance to genuine trees. Their very brilliance, their vivid colors and their crystal-like patterns, made them the object of rapacious collection, and many thousand tons were removed before the area became a national park. Today, severe penalties are imposed on anyone attempting to remove even the tiniest piece.

The "Painted Desert" of that early description takes its name from the minerals and impurities the rocks contain. Iron compounds produce an endless variety of subtly different shades of red and brown; organic material results in dark grays and black. Weathering is important too: brilliance and freshness of color also depend on how long a layer of rock has been exposed to the weather.

Those first explorers failed to mention a third feature of the area, now carefully preserved since the national park was established – there has been human habitation here for over 2,000 years, as the ruins of Indian villages, potsherds and petroglyphs bear witness.

REDWOOD
California

Redwood National Park preserves the celebrated coast redwoods of northern California. By no means all of them, however, since nearly two million trees originally grew here before westward expansion brought the frontier settlers in the 1820s and 1830s. Today, barely half – perhaps far fewer – still survive. The problem has been that the coast redwood makes excellent lumber, unlike the giant sequoias of the Sierra Nevada. Redwood neither shrinks nor decays; it is straight-grained and easy to work. With qualities like these, and with the ever-increasing demand for manufactured goods of all kinds during the last and present centuries, how could the redwoods resist the advance of the loggers? It was only after many years of effort, with persistent resistance from lumber companies, that some protection was won – and even now logging continues outside the boundaries of the national park.

Among the trees that will be conserved, however, is the tallest in the world: a 367.8-foot specimen discovered on the banks of Redwood Creek in 1964. Coast redwoods are also among the oldest trees in the world, some specimens living 2,200 years.

Once, millions of years ago, when dinosaurs inhabited our planet, and the climate was warmer and wetter than it is now, redwoods grew throughout the northern hemisphere. It is the low-lying coastal fringe of northern California, no more than 30 miles wide and 3,000 feet high, that today most nearly reproduces those conditions. Coast redwoods thrive amid the heavy rains and sudden fogs of this area, growing in dense, cloistered groups; the ground carpeted with needles and moss, the sky almost hidden by the overlapping branches, their tiny leaves a delicate green.

There can be no disputing that these magnificent and awesome trees are the first priority for every visitor to Redwood National Park. But there is much else to observe. Every spring and fall brings migrating birds. On land there are Roosevelt elk, mountain lion and blacktail deer; gray whales, porpoises, seals and sea lions in the ocean; beaver, mink and river otters in the freshwater rivers. The park is, in short, a paradise; a paradise that man and nature can share peacefully, where the natural world can thrive and man can be at rest.

ROCKY MOUNTAIN
Colorado

If any one area can be said to symbolize the great American outdoors, Rocky Mountain National Park must surely be that place. Within its 263,000 acres are to be found no less than 65 peaks of more than 10,000 feet. And amid this towering splendor – the product of volcanic activity over some 60 million years and then of several great ice ages whose glaciers formed and cut the land to its present shape – there is abundant wildlife, carpets of wild flowers, forests, and cool, high, mountain lakes.

This is a truly fascinating environment, for here there are no less than four distinct climates, each succeeding the other as one climbs higher. At the lowest level, the Plains Zone (4,000 to 6,000 feet), there are relatively few trees, and the characteristic landscape is short grass. The Montane Zone (6,000 to 9,000 feet) supports alders, willows, ponderosa pines and the celebrated Colorado blue spruce, elsewhere a popular ornamental tree. Above this lies the Subalpine Zone (9,000 to 11,500 feet), where the Engelmann spruce grows alongside numerous wild flowers – among them marsh marigolds, primroses and Colorado blue columbines – Colorado's state flower. Finally, the Alpine Zone is reached. The trees stop at 11,500 feet – although in sheltered spots a thin line may stretch higher still – giving way to Alpine flowers, grasses, mosses and lichens. The Trail Ridge Road, the highest through road in North America, provides an unparalleled opportunity to study environments normally inaccessible to all but climbers and the hardiest walkers. Beyond the treeline the marked trails must be followed. The Alpine ecosystem is fragile, and even a short diversion from the path may cause irrecoverable damage.

The best way to explore the park, and to take in its full majesty, is undoubtedly on foot. There are over 370 miles of trails, and overnight trips (a permit is required) take you into the back country, far from the roads and the developed areas. But even if you choose to do your exploring by car, you will surely be overawed by nature's work.

SAMOA
American Samoa

The newest of America's fifty national parks and, except for Hot Springs, the smallest at 9,000 acres, this national park was created in 1988 to preserve a unique, undisturbed paleo-tropical rain forest, similar to those found in Asia. The Territory of American Samoa is north of New Zealand and east of the Solomons, about 2,300 miles south-southwest of Honolulu, the only American territory south of the Equator. In addition to the rain forest, the park also includes seven miles of coral reefs protecting white, sandy beaches. The reefs, off the volcanic island of Tutuila, are teeming with exotic life, including hawks-bill and green sea turtles, surgeonfish, parrotfish, octopus, sea snails and palolo worms, which the native Polynesians catch for food. The forest supports a variety of wildlife, including the Pacific boa, gecko lizard, flying fox, sheath-tail bat, rats and pigs. But most spectacular of all is the park's fifty-five species of birds.

The five volcanic islands and two coral atolls that comprise American Samoa became a US Territory in 1900 through a treaty with Germany and the United Kingdom, after which the local chiefs ceded the seventy-seven square miles to the United States. It was administered by the Navy until 1951, when jurisdiction was transferred to the Interior Department. The citizens of the Territory, who are all considered American nationals, began electing their own governors, and a single member of Congress in 1978. Samoa National Park was created in parts of the islands of Tutuila and Ta´u from communally owned land.

SEQUOIA AND KINGS CANYON
California

These two national parks, administered as one unit, lie in the heart of the Sierra Nevada – the great mountain range that runs for 400 miles, northwest to southeast, through eastern California. The land is the product of a great geological upheaval, in which the earth split along a fault. One block was lifted up and tilted westward over the neighboring land, forming a high mountain range. The resulting steep escarpment on the eastern edge of the Sierra Nevada, where the land rises sheer out of the desert, is a classic and dramatic example of fault-block building.

But the impact of geological forces was not yet complete. One result of the tilting was that the rivers flowed faster and their cutting force increased. Together with the great glaciers that covered the land, they carved out spectacular canyons, sculpted huge, natural amphitheatres, called cirques, and scooped out basins that later became lakes.

The natural phenomenon for which these two national parks are justly most celebrated is, however, young by the geological clock, though ancient in human terms. The giant sequoia (the tree is named in honor of the great Cherokee chief) is now found only on the western slopes of the Sierra Nevada, growing in isolated groves above about 5,000 feet. Some 40,000 specimens remain: a substantial number one might think, until one recalls the depredations of the loggers who, in the last four decades of the 19th century, wantonly destroyed entire forests. The establishment of the national park in 1890 put a stop to this vandalism, but not before at least two trees even bigger than the celebrated General Sherman Tree had been lost.

The General Sherman, in Giant Forest on the western side of Sequoia National Park, is one of the largest and most ancient living things on our planet. Some 2,500 years old – it was already a mature tree at the time of Christ – it stands 272 feet tall, with a trunk 36 feet in diameter. Here, in the beauty and majesty of these national parks, you may enjoy scenery as stunning as you will find anywhere on the continent and can wonder at these timeless marvels of nature.

SHENANDOAH
Virginia

Artefacts and burial mounds left by the earliest settlers on the Blue Ridge Mountains have been found. But otherwise, nothing remains now to tell us of what was probably several thousand years of human habitation. More recently, the first European settlement began in the Shenandoah Valley in 1716, and in little more than two centuries the land and its plentiful resources were exploited and worn out. Only dedication, determination and vision – a magnificent vision of how the land might be restored to something of its former glory – were able to prevent complete disaster.

Settlement began harmlessly enough, with small numbers of immigrants coming along the Shenandoah River from Pennsylvania and farming the low-lying land. It was in the 19th century, when the lowlands were full and population pressures were increasing, that the damage began. Agriculture moved up the mountains, but winning a living from high ground is hard. Land must be cleared and centuries-old trees felled; wildlife is hunted and destroyed; sheep and cattle are grazed. By the early years of the present century, much of the land had been stripped of its goodness; if not by agriculture then by mining for copper, iron and manganese. The farmers and miners moved on, leaving behind them a blighted landscape and a depressed and poverty-stricken people.

After years of legal wrangling – and many years before that of campaigning by people such as George Freeman Pollock, who owned 5,000 acres of mountain top and the celebrated Skyland Resort – a national park was established in 1935. The remaining inhabitants were resettled, Skyline Drive along the ridge of the mountains was built, and the stage was set for an almost unique experiment – an attempt to restore an area to its former natural state. Nearly fifty years later, the experiment seems to have worked, and worked better than could perhaps ever have been foreseen. Over 95 percent of the park is now forested, and there are some one hundred species of tree. And many animals, long since driven from their former home, have now returned: deer, turkey, bear and bobcat among them.

Shenandoah National Park is a true success story, a living witness to the value of the conservation ideal.

THEODORE ROOSEVELT
North Dakota

One does not normally associate those who hold the highest office in the land – that of President of the United States of America – with the outdoor life. Whatever the circumstances of their upbringing, politicians today and for many decades past have seemed more at home in the smoke-filled rooms of caucus meetings than under the wide-open skies, where man can sense his insignificant place in the scheme of things.

But it was not thus with Theodore Roosevelt, president of the United States from 1901 to 1909. Nearly twenty years before he entered the doors of the White House he came to the North Dakota Badlands to hunt bison. Even then, the area's "dismal beauty," as he once described it, must have exerted a strong pull, since before he returned East he had become a partner in the Maltese Cross Ranch. Just a few months later, it proved a literal lifesaver. In February 1884, Roosevelt's wife and his mother died on the same day. The young politician retreated to his Badlands ranch to overcome his grief and recharge his spirits.

Roosevelt spent two and a half years in North Dakota. Although his interest in his ranches (he founded his own, the Elkhorn, while remaining a partner in the Maltese Cross) later diminished, it was at this time that he developed the concern for the environment, and for the proper use of resources, concerns which characterized his presidency. In his White House years he established the Forest Service, signed the Antiquities Act, proclaimed fifteen sites of historic interest and also set up five national parks. In his many writings, too, Roosevelt did much to promote the conservationist cause.

What was the land that so attracted him? It is typical Badlands scenery: bizarre shapes sculpted by the action of water cutting through soft strata, towering out of a dry land sparsely covered with grass and sagebrush. The land seems unforgiving and unwelcoming, but there is much animal life, including bighorn, bison and antelope, once hunted to near-extinction but now reintroduced by the National Park Service. Theodore Roosevelt would undoubtedly have approved.

VIRGIN ISLANDS
Virgin Islands

Tourism, and all the trappings of late-20th century "civilization," are a constant threat to the islands of the Caribbean. The Virgin Islands National Park is a courageous – and successful – attempt to preserve an unspoiled environment and a delicate ecological balance.

The island of St. John, the smallest of the three inhabited US Virgin Islands (there are nearly 60 other uninhabited islets), which lie between Puerto Rico and the British Virgin Islands, is the site for the national park. The park area covers about three-quarters of the island – and a significant amount of ocean, too. It is in the ocean that the park's most intriguing and beautiful natural feature is to be found: its coral reefs. The coral fringes the white sand beaches, protecting them from winter waves. It grows from rock outcrops and small rocky cays (islands), in a profusion of endlessly fascinating colors and textures, and is home to many different fish that gleam and glint in the clear, bright waters.

On land, signs of the once-important sugar industry are vanishing rapidly. The sugar plantations were developed by Danish settlers, the first formal white inhabitants, in the late 18th century. Slaves were imported from West Africa to work the land. But in 1848 emancipation brought the great estates to an end, and now the original, subtropical, moist forest is returning. At Leinster Bay, the Annaberg sugar mill and plantation area have been partially restored, and in Reef Bay the ruined estate house and the steam-powered sugar mill can be seen. Elsewhere, on the southern and eastern slopes of the island, there is subtropical dry forest, and on the southern and eastern shore conditions are desert-like, with turks head and dildo cacti.

VOYAGEURS
Minnesota

The "voyageurs" (the word is French for travelers) who gave their name to this national park were a unique group of frontiersmen. Their commodity was fur. Their means of transport was birch-bark canoe. Their strength and character were legendary. And their special knowledge was of the myriad waterways of northwestern North America and of the customs of the indigenous Indian inhabitants.

These men were middlemen in the fur trade – the trade that more than any other established the economic viability of northern North America. Pelts were in demand in Europe – in great demand, and the business was a profitable one. The voyageurs traveled between the Indian trappers of the northwest and the fur-dealers of Montreal, bringing pelts to the one and manufactured items to the other in exchange. It was a tough and dangerous business. Voyageurs would leave Grand Portage and Fort William on Lake Superior in spring, as soon as the ice and snow began to melt, and make for the interior, often traveling for as long as sixteen hours a day. Their exchanges made, they returned south before the autumn snows began. The voyageurs were independent, colorful, resolute men, cheerful and indomitable, prepared to accept great physical discomfort and willing to risk their lives in the pursuit of their trade.

The national park founded to commemorate them lies along one edge of the Voyageurs Highway, the water route from Lake Superior to Lake of the Woods, on the eastern edge of Ontario Province. It is a watery world. There are literally hundreds of ponds, lakes and streams, gathered in depressions left by the mighty continental glaciers – sheets of ice no less than two miles thick – that covered the area within the last million years. Travel is by boat or float plane, or on skis in winter. Here there are osprey, eagle and great blue heron, cormorants, mergansers, loon and kingfishers. There are timber wolves and coyote. And of course there remain the beavers, still building their ponds as they have for centuries past, their coats, however, no longer here the goal of hunters.

WIND CAVE
South Dakota

Wind Cave National Park takes its name from a curious, natural phenomenon, for which changes in atmospheric pressure are said to be responsible. When the pressure in the open air is greater than that inside the cave, the wind blows into the cave. When it is less outside than in, the wind reverses direction and blows out. It is said that the two local cowboys who discovered the cave in 1881 did so because they heard a strange, whistling sound – the noise of wind escaping through a blowhole.

Inside the cave there are one-and-a-quarter miles of passages and caverns to explore. A further 32 miles have been discovered, but are left in their natural state, and there may well be more: no one knows how far Wind Cave actually does extend. The fascinating and beautiful feature of the cave are the boxwork patterns that cover its limestone walls. These are the result of calcium carbonate, or calcite. The calcite was deposited in countless tiny cracks and crevices in the limestone; the limestone slowly wore away and a fragile network of crystal, shimmering red and pink, was left.

There is also much to see above ground, where the park is a fascinating example of the original prairie ecosystem. There are many prairie grasses and, in spring and summer, wild flowers. Of the park's many animals, the bison and the prairie dog are the most interesting. Bison once lived on the prairie in the thousands. Virtually wiped out by the end of the last century, they are now returning, due to the care of conservationists who have built up the stock over many decades. The prairie dog population was similarly depleted. At the turn of the century there were some 400 million of these swift little rodents. Today, they are virtually extinct, although two towns – as packs of prairie dogs are called – do survive here.

WRANGELL-ST. ELIAS
Alaska

If you like superlatives, you'll love Wrangell-St. Elias. It is the largest of the fifty US national parks – equal to four Yellowstones – and if the adjoining Kluane National Park, in Canada's Yukon Territory, is added in, it is easy to understand why the World Heritage List refers to their combined 27,875 square miles as "North America's Mountain Kingdom." The king of its hills is the lofty Mt. St. Elias, at 18,808 feet, the second highest in the United States and fourth highest in North America. Nine of the sixteen highest peaks in the United States, seven of which are more than 15,000 feet high, are within the park. Also within its boundaries is the Bagley Icefield, ninety-miles long and three-quarters-of-a-mile thick, the biggest in North America below the Arctic Circle. It has spawned more than a hundred glaciers, one of which, the Malaspina, is almost as big as the State of Connecticut. And while many travelers say that the landscapes of Wrangell-St. Elias are in a class with the Himalayas, the park also includes coastal beaches.

Although sparsely covered with vegetation, the park is home to a wide variety of wildlife, including mountain goats and Dall sheep, caribou, moose, black and grizzly bears. It also has a substantial herd of bison, descended from animals introduced in the Copper River and Chitina River valleys in 1950 and again in 1962. The park's rivers are also a spawning ground for salmon, and its ponds provide nesting areas for the rare trumpeter swan. It is also a major stopping place for migratory birds.

Mt. St. Elias was the first landmark spotted by the Russian explorer Vitus Bering when he discovered northwestern America in 1741, and it was he who named it for the saint whose feast day it was. No one climbed the mountain until 1897, and very few explored the area until several years later, when the Kennecott Copper Company was formed to mine the minerals there. The mines closed down in the 1930s and the two settlements the company established became ghost towns. But even before Bering sailed past, and long before the miners arrived, the coastline was the site of Indian fishing villages, some of which seem to have been thriving in prehistoric times. It became a center of a different kind of human activity in 1980, when Congress established Mt. St. Elias National Park. But it is still a virgin wilderness, difficult to reach except by plane. On the other hand, for backpackers, hikers, campers, fishermen, cross-country skiers and others who love the great outdoors, Wrangell-St. Elias is the ultimate experience.

YELLOWSTONE
Idaho, Montana, Wyoming

Yellowstone National Park is a peaceful land, a huge tract in which wildlife can roam undisturbed, and man is the visitor. There are 3,500 square miles of wilderness – home for bear, elk, bison, moose, antelope and many other mammal and bird species. There are many natural landscape beauties – among them the Grand Canyon of the Yellowstone, no less than 24 miles long and 1,200 feet deep.

Here are some 10,000 geysers, pots of boiling mud, fumaroles (steam vents) and sulphur springs: the visible, outward sign of seething, liquid rocks buried deep within the earth. Geysers occur because deep underground liquid rock, or volcanic magma, and a water source meet. The water is heated, and steam and hot water are forced upward through faults in the rocks. Eventually the pressure underground becomes so great that steam and water spurt out in gigantic jets. The entire Yellowstone basin is a caldera; a huge bowl created after a mammoth volcanic eruption some 600,000 years ago.

The most celebrated of all the geysers at Yellowstone is "Old Faithful" – so-called because of the frequency of its eruptions, which happen every sixty-four-and-a-half minutes on average, although intervals of as little as 30, and as much as 90 minutes, are not uncommon. The waters reach a height of 115 to 150 feet, some 12,000 gallons being expelled in only a few minutes. Here, and at many other geysers in the park – Mammoth Hot Springs, New Highland Terrace and White Elephant Back Terrace, for instance – beautiful terraces of travertine, often etched in unusual shapes, form a graceful background to the steaming waters. The travertine is a form of calcium carbonate dissolved in the waters that carry it to the surface, and left behind after they evaporate.

Here in Yellowstone, there is permanent evidence – evidence one can never forget – that the earth is its own master and is not for taming by man.

YOSEMITE
California

This was one of the places where the conservationist idea first took root – deservedly so, and not a moment too soon. Deservedly because, of all the beauty and majesty contained in all the national parks scattered across the nation, Yosemite represents, at least in the opinion of many, the pinnacle. And not a moment too soon, because a scarce ten years after white men finally expelled the Ahwahneechee Indians from their home, a true tourist trade had already begun to threaten Yosemite's unique splendors.

Thousands of years ago, glacial ice carved the awesome landscape we see today. Glaciers broadened the canyon on the Merced River to form the Yosemite Valley, seven miles long and almost two miles wide, scouring and carving through the joints in the weaker rock, but leaving the harder rocks intact. Preeminent among these is the aptly named El Capitan, its sheer walls 3,600 feet high, the largest block of granite on earth. Glaciers also formed the spectacular waterfalls that drop, unimpeded by intervening ledges, down the sheer canyon walls. The greatest of these is the Upper Yosemite Falls, the highest on the continent. They fall free to a ledge 1,430 feet below and then drop a further 1,000 feet.

If Yosemite ended here, these would be splendors enough. But there is also the Grand Canyon of the Tuolumne River further north, whose walls retained their V-shape despite the force of the glacial ice. There are the sequoia groves, including Mariposa Grove, where the Grizzly Giant vies with General Sherman in Sequoia National Park for the title of oldest tree. And there is the fascinating Alpine scenery of Tuolumne Meadows and the high country, with abundant wild flowers and wildlife.

For visitors prepared to leave their cars and take to their feet Yosemite offers much. A half-mile hike is all that is needed to enter a new world – a world in which man is dwarfed and awed, yet renewed as well.

ZION
Utah

Centerpiece of the Zion National Park, without question, is the canyon of the Virgin River, an extraordinary tribute to the powerful and persistent force of water. For it is water, seeking a path through the rock, that has created the immense, perpendicular walls of the canyon, half a mile high and normally about a quarter-mile apart. At one point the spectacular Narrows – the gap between the walls – closes to a mere 20 feet, far less than the average city street. One can hardly believe that this normally sluggish water could develop such force and create such amazing works of nature. But three million tons of rock are carried downstream to the confluence with the Colorado every year, and after the summer rains the quiet stream becomes a raging torrent.

What, besides the canyon itself (along which hikes are possible), awaits the visitor in this national park? There is fishing, horseback-riding and, above all, a wide variety of walks and hikes to suit people of all energies. There is also the chance to study the fascinating geology of the area, for the rocks here are a record of changes over many millions of years, and there are fossil records of great reptiles, the first birds and some early mammals. The vegetation repays interest, too. Along the floor of the canyon there is riparian woodland; above the cliffs woodland and open land dotted with shrubs; and finally high country, with ponderosa pine and Douglas fir. Many species of bird live throughout the year in the park, but migrate for the winter from the high country down to the canyons.

And the curious name? How did that come about? Joseph Black, a Mormon pioneer who lived on the outer edge of the canyon, named it Zion, which means "the heavenly city of God." Brigham Young, the Mormon leader, disagreed. He called it *Not* Zion, but Black's original and more positive description has held sway.

Bass Harbor Lighthouse (facing page) is located on a remote, wild headland on Mount Desert Island, Acadia National Park. The lighthouse, which watches over some of Maine's most treacherous coastline, is at its most picturesque at sunset.

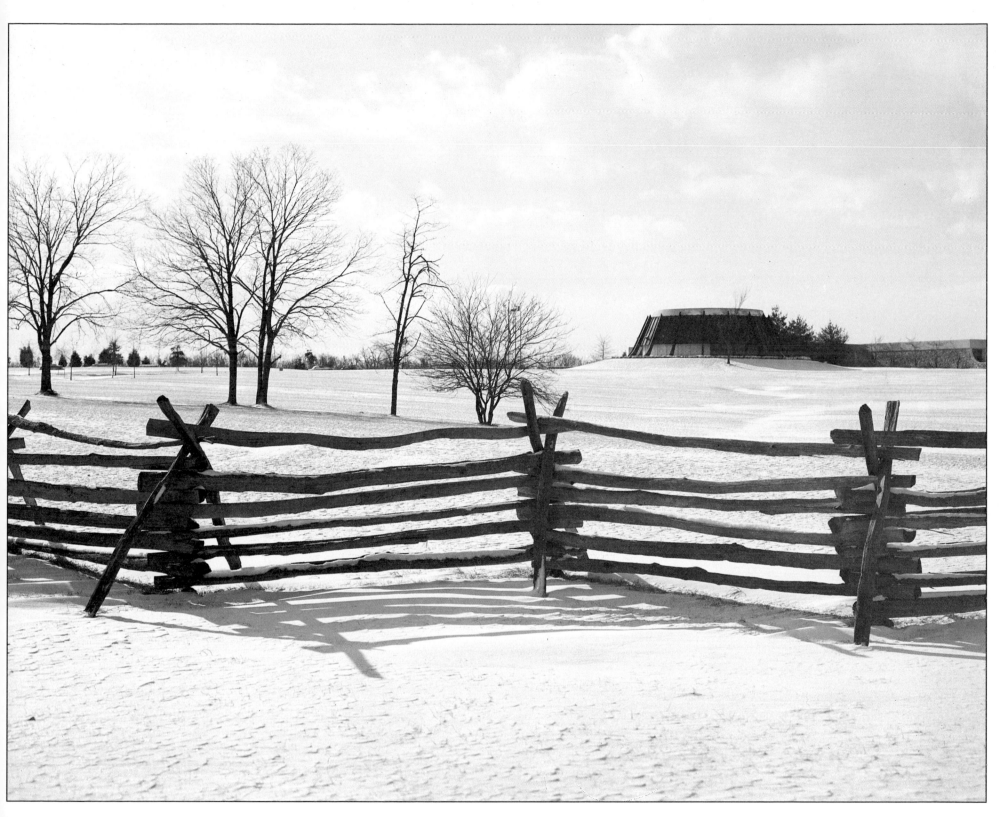

New Market Battlefield Park (above), in northwestern Virginia, is located on the site where one of the most dramatic battles of the Civil War took place, and boasts the state's finest Civil War museum. Facing page: an elegant, colonial-style home, set against the snow-clad landscape of Virginia's Shenandoah National Park.

Great Smoky Mountains National Park (these pages) covers an area of 800 square miles high in the Appalachian Mountains and straddles the border between Tennessee and North Carolina. The scenery at Cades Cove (above), one of the open valleys characteristic of the park, is particularly lovely in fall, when the leaves on the deciduous trees turn a beautiful golden color.

The smoke-like mist from which Great Smoky Mountains National Park takes its name shrouds the upper reaches of the mountains above Newfound Gap Road (above). The scenic, winding road passes through Newfound Gap, offering magnificent views of the park's spectacular, densely-wooded mountain scenery. Facing page: Grotto Falls near Gatlinburg, one of the prettiest waterfalls in Great Smoky Mountains National Park.

Everglades National Park was established in 1934 to preserve a part of the unique, fast-disappearing subtropical wilderness area that once covered much of the Florida peninsula. The plant and animal life in the park is diverse, ranging from lush pond vegetation (above) to dense, almost eerie, cypress swamps (facing page). Overleaf: sunset in Everglades National Park, when its magical, timeless beauty is most apparent.

Maho Bay (above) and Trunk Bay (facing page) are just two of the idyllic beaches found in Virgin Islands National Park, which, established in 1956, is famous for its Carib Indian relics. Overleaf left: Santa Elena Canyon, one of the three huge canyons carved by the Rio Grande in Big Bend National Park, Texas. Overleaf right: hardy desert vegetation around Hunter Peak, in Guadalupe Mountains National Park, southwest Texas.

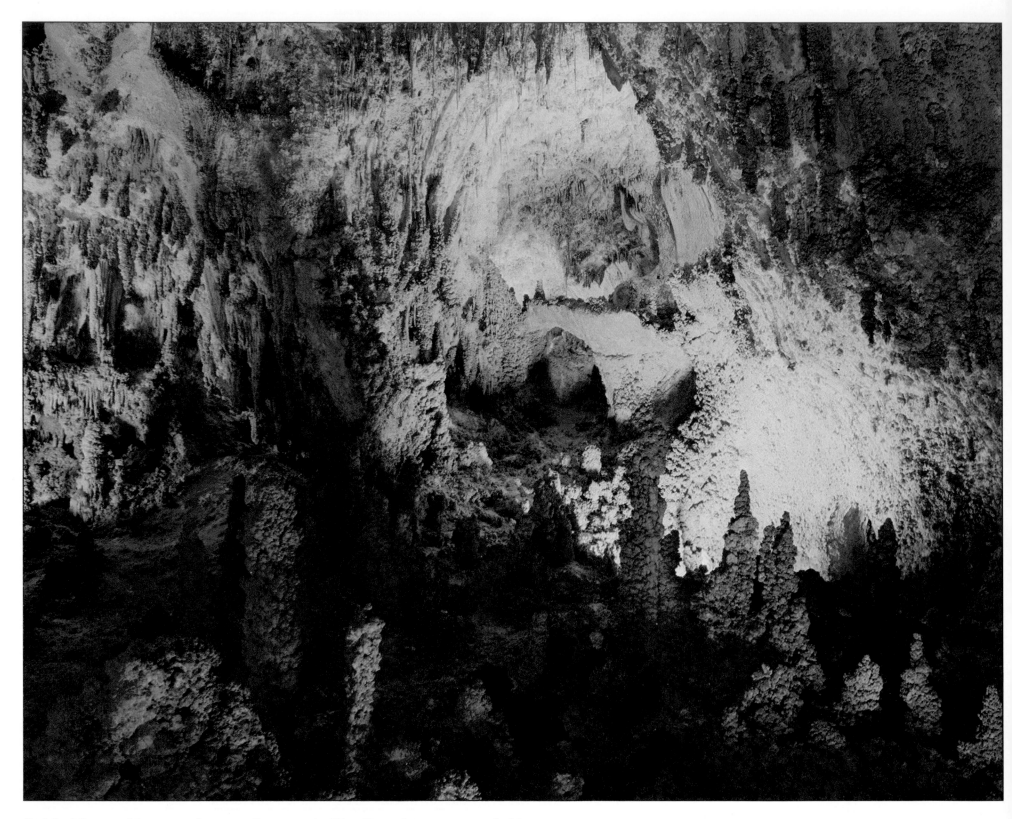

Carlsbad Caverns (these pages), among the greatest of New Mexico's treasures, are hidden beneath the foothills of the Guadalupe Mountains. The huge caverns – a wonderland of giant underground galleries filled with rock formations of every imaginable shape, color, and size, that were millions of years in the making – were designated a National Park in 1930.

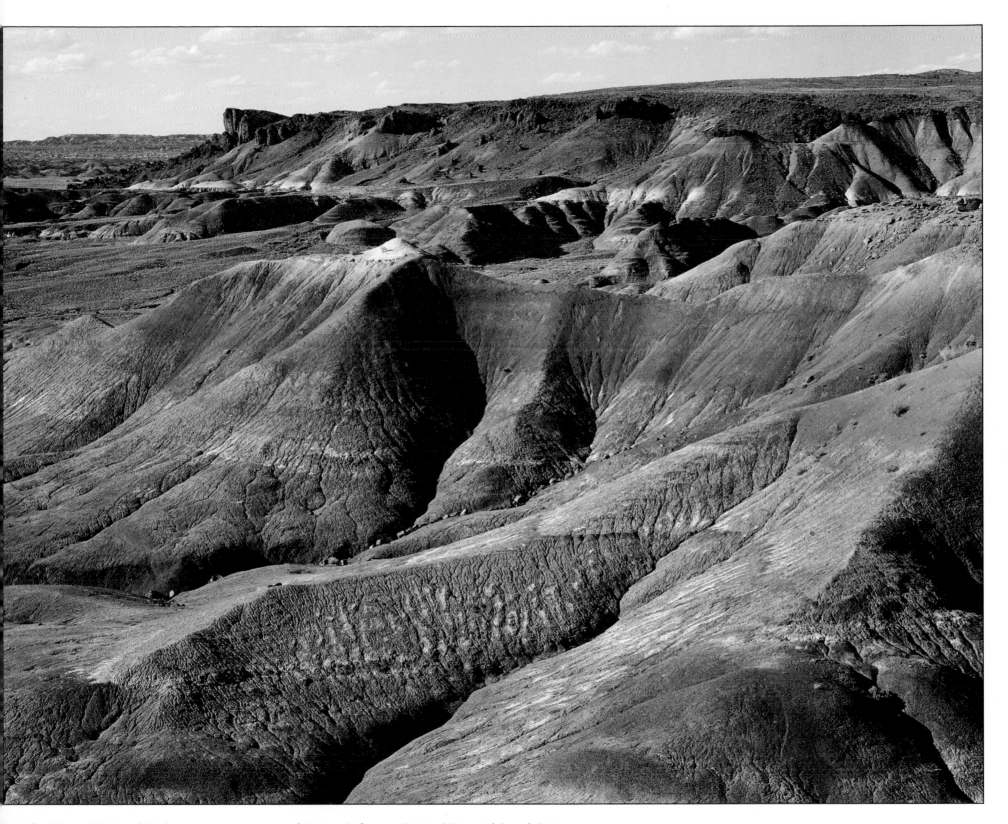

Petrified Forest National Park encompasses some of Arizona's famous Painted Desert (above). It is better-known, however, for its collection of petrified wood (facing page), which is the finest anywhere in the world. The logs are the remains of trees that grew in the area over 160-million years ago. Floods covered the trees in mud and volcanic ash, and over time the minerals that they carried were absorbed by the tree cells, converting them to stone.

The twelfth-century cave dwellings in Colorado's Mesa Verde National Park (these pages) are
evidence of the sophisticated Indian civilization that once existed in the region. The caves
themselves, and the fascinating objects discovered in them, help build up a picture of what life
was like for the inhabitants. Cliff Palace (facing page), the first of the cliff dwellings to be
discovered, is the largest and most famous.

Few of America's national parks are more famous than Grand Canyon National Park, in Arizona. The canyon, which at points is over eighteen miles wide and one mile deep, is counted among the seven natural wonders of the world. Views of the canyon from Moran Point (above) and Yaki Point (facing page) – both located on the South Rim – exemplify its majestic beauty.

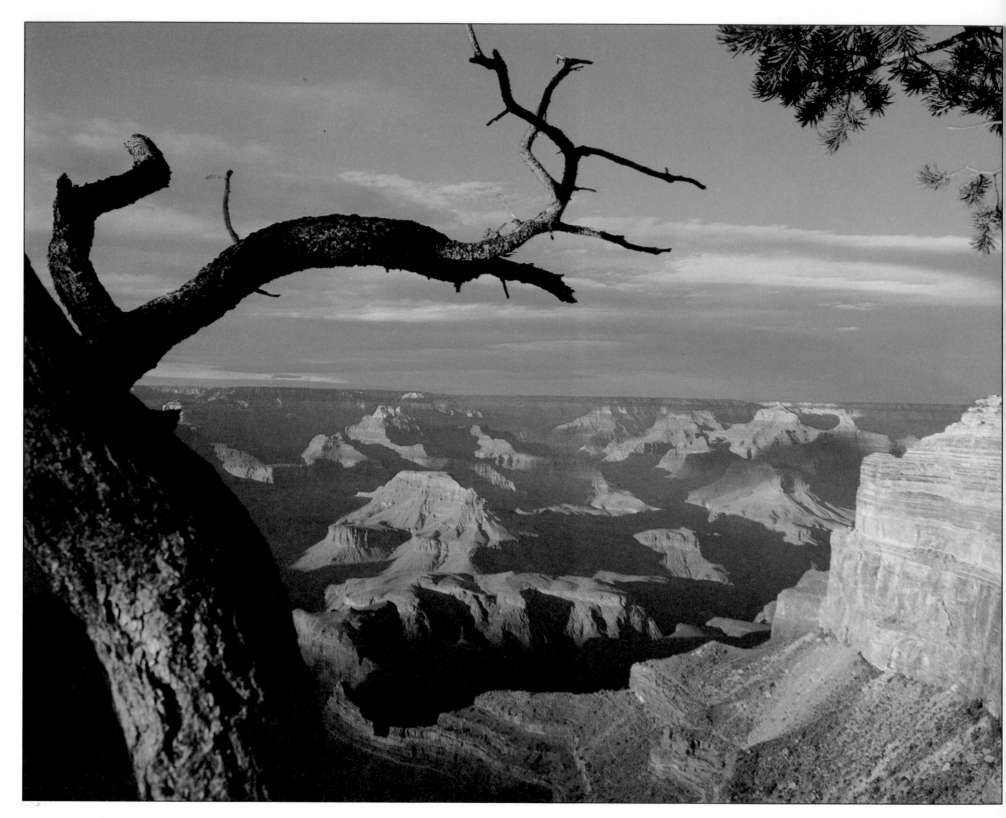

Panoramic views of the Grand Canyon (these pages) reveal its awesome beauty. The view from
Hopi Point (facing page) brings the sheer scale and variety of the canyon into perspective.

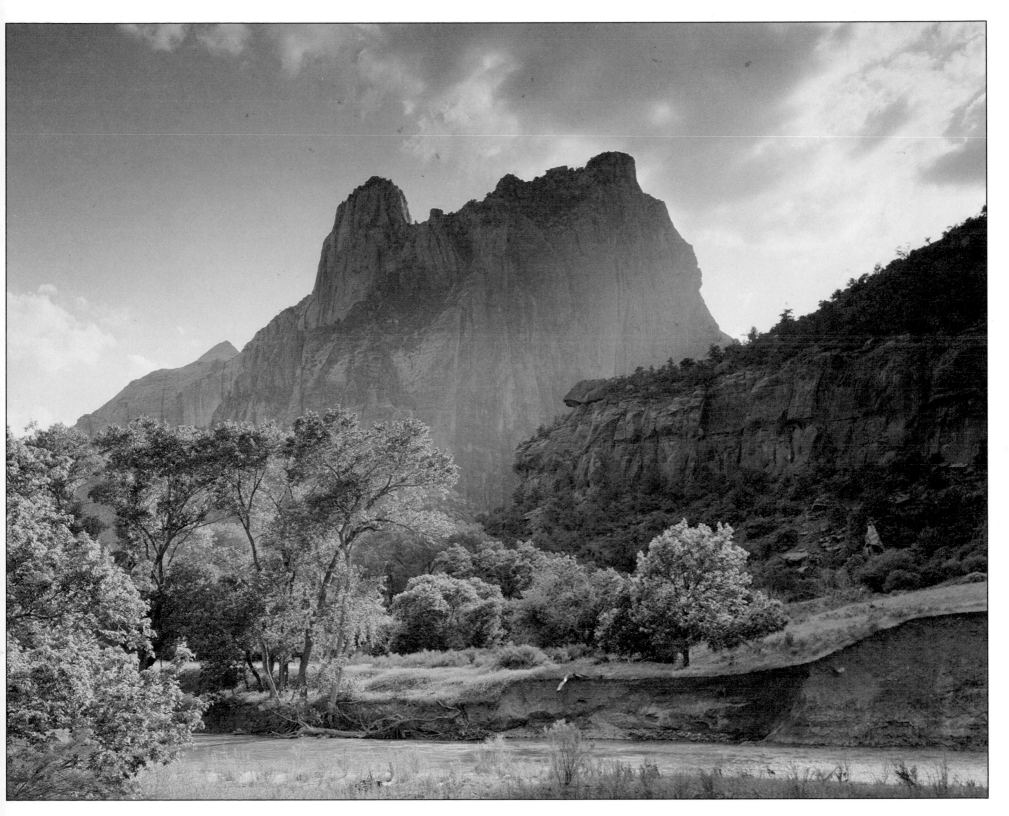

Zion Canyon, in southern Utah's Zion National Park, is famed for its monumental rock formations, each of which is evocatively named. The Watchman (facing page), seen from the waters of the North Fork of the Virgin River, and the Sentinel (above), both tower over the surrounding landscape.

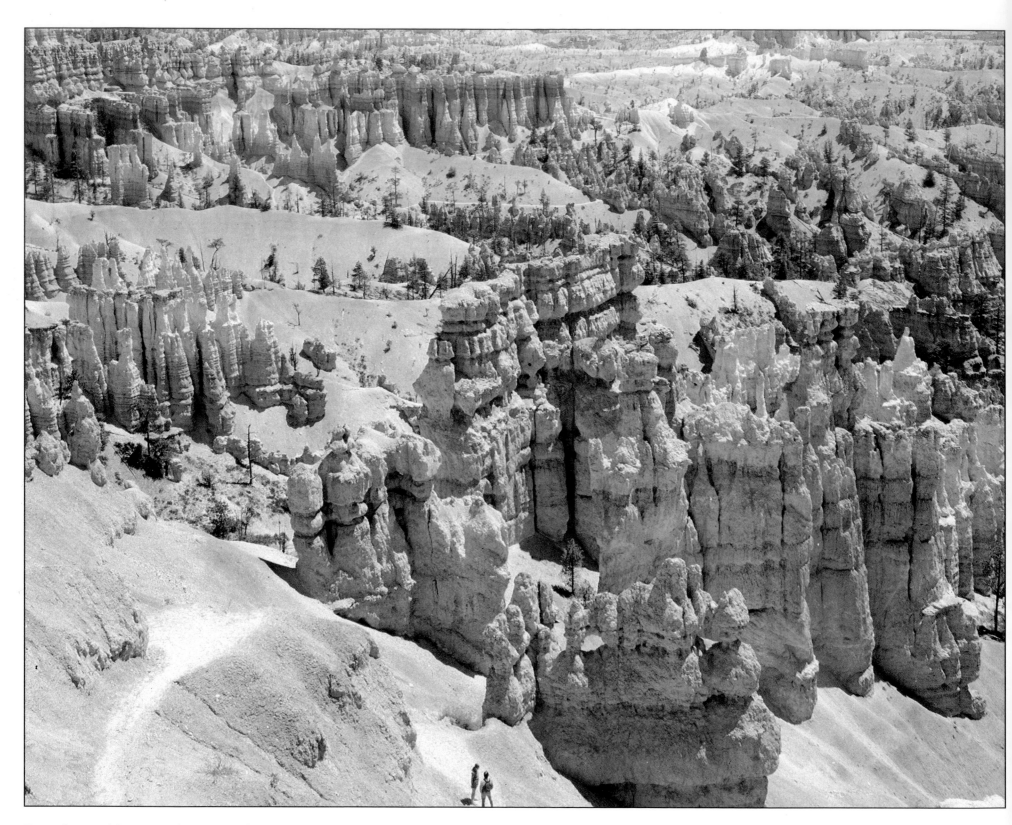

Bryce Canyon (these pages) – named after the nineteenth-century settler Ebenezer Bryce – is one of the glories of Utah. Over centuries the soft and hard rocks of the canyon have been shaped by the elements, and strange, twisting rock formations of extraordinary beauty, like those in the Queen's Garden (above) and Fairyland Trail (facing page), have been created. The canyon, which is located in the southwestern part of the state, was designated a national park in 1928.

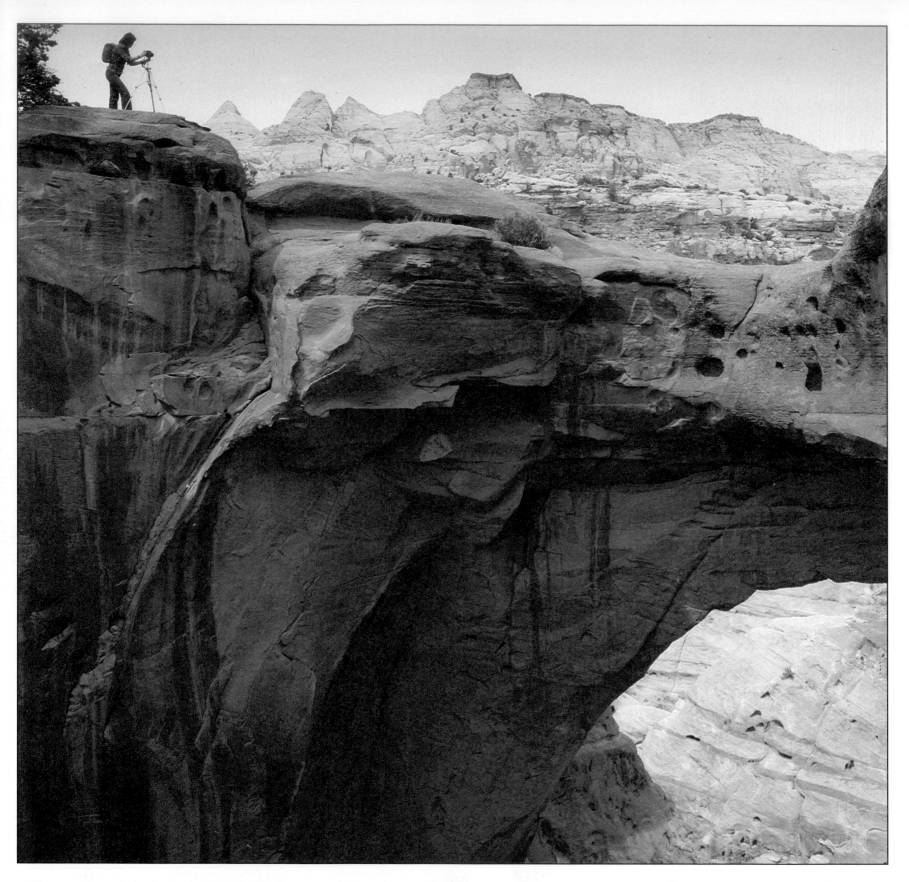

The view through Hickman Natural Bridge (facing page) reveals the spectacular, untamed
landscape for which Utah's Capitol Reef National Park is famed. Though larger than both Bryce
Canyon and Zion national parks combined, Capitol Reef is less accessible, and therefore less well
known. Above: the graceful sweep of Cassidy Arch.

Delicate Arch (facing page), in Utah's Arches National Park, reaches over 100 feet in height. Like many of the other rock formations found in the state, the magnificent, unsupported arch – which has been dubbed Schoolmarm's Britches by locals – was created by wind and rain erosion. Above: Big Spring Canyon Overlook in Canyonlands National Park, Utah.

Double Arch (above), North Window (facing page top left) and South Window (center right) are three of the four stone arches that make up the famous Windows Section of Arches National Park, in Utah. Other features, elsewhere in the park, include Devils Garden (top right), The Organ (bottom right) and the sheer walls of South Park Avenue (bottom left).

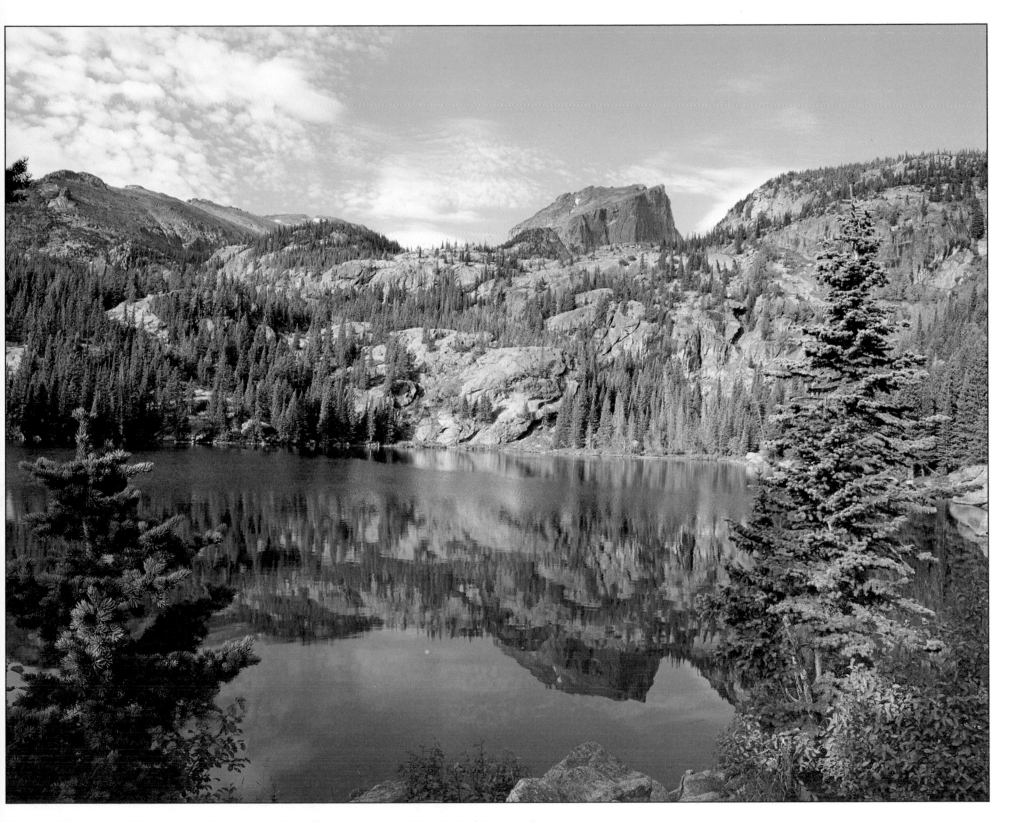

The jewel-like lakes of Colorado, such as Dream Lake (facing page) and Bear Lake (above and overleaf left), reflect the majesty of their settings and are a feature of Rocky Mountains National Park. Overleaf right: the still waters of Beaver Ponds, Hidden Valley.

Many of California's natural beauties are preserved in Sequoia National Park (these pages).
Though the ancient redwoods (facing page) are undoubtedly the most popular of the park's
attractions, it also offers other sites of great significance such as Monarch Lakes, Rainbow
Mountain and Mineral Peak (above).

Kings Canyon National Park lies side by side with Sequoia National Park, at the center of the Sierra Nevada, in eastern central California. Like its near neighbour, Kings Canyon encompasses some superb mountain scenery, like that at Junction Ridge (above). Facing page: the meandering Merced River weaving its way through steep-sided Yosemite Valley, in Yosemite National Park, California.

From Glacier Point (above), visitors to Yosemite National Park can enjoy magnificent, panoramic views of Upper Yosemite Valley. The valley, created many thousands of years ago by glacial movement, offers some of California's finest scenery. Facing page: a view of Yosemite Valley, from Washburn Point, showing Nevada (upper) Falls and Vernal (lower) Falls.

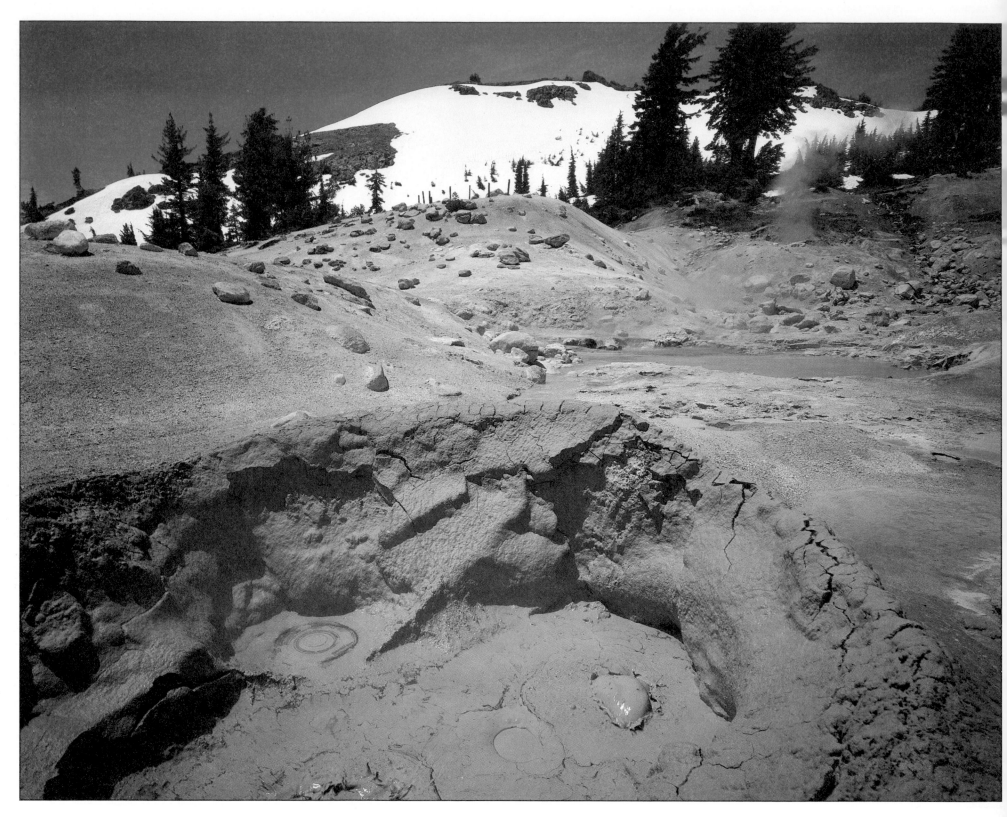

California's Lassen Volcanic National Park (these pages), which occupies an area of 165 square miles in the southernmost part of the Cascade Range, boasts a spectacular hydrothermal area. Bumpass Hell (facing page) with its numerous boiling mudpots (above), pools, and fumaroles creates a fascinating, almost unearthly scene.

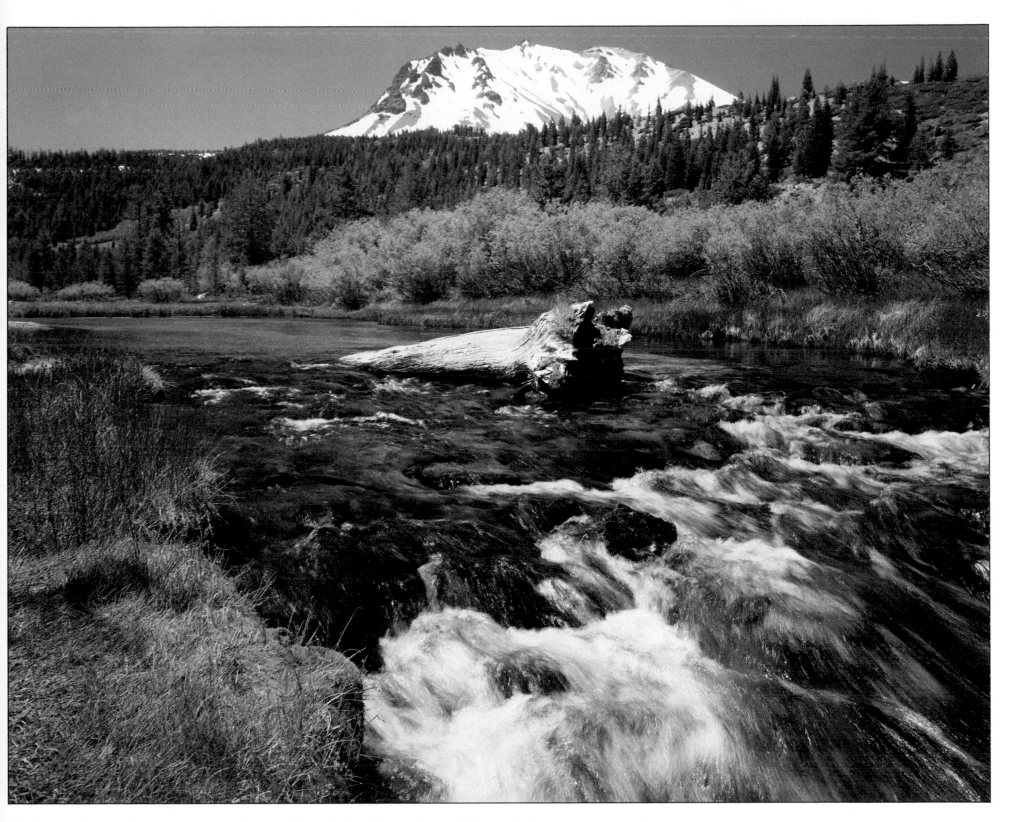

The Painted Dunes (facing page) – smooth, undulating cinder hills – in Lassen Volcanic Park, where only the hardiest of plants survive, present a dramatic contrast to the verdant banks of rushing Hat Creek (above).

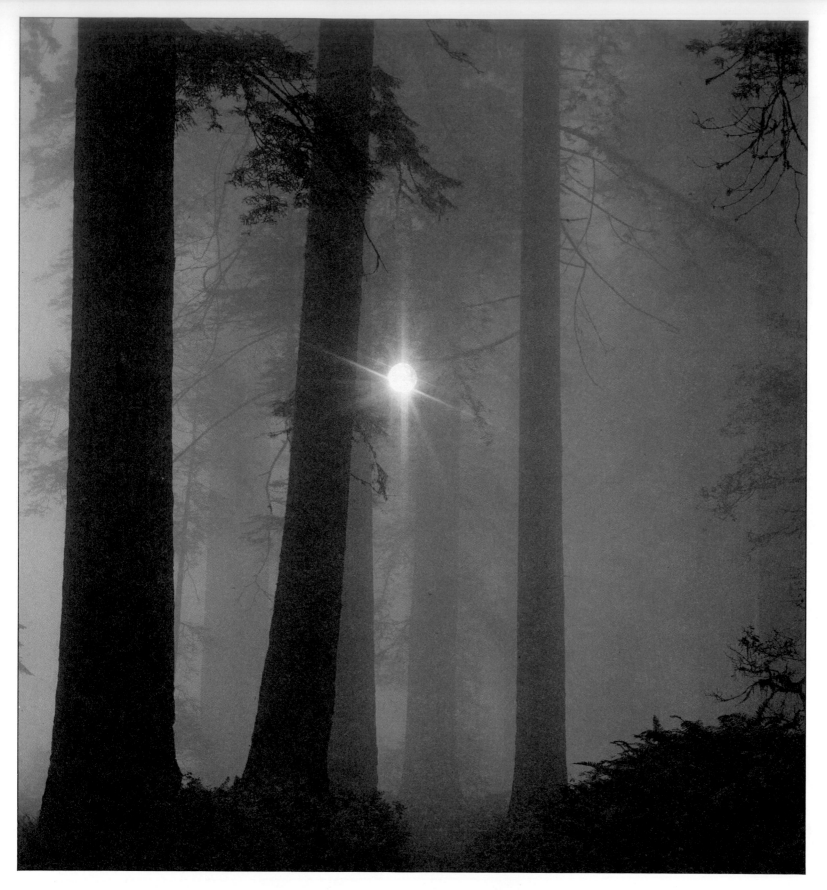

A forty-mile span of northern California's Pacific coastline has been preserved in Redwood National Park (these pages). The park's scenery, which includes dense forests of redwood such as Lady Bird Johnson Grove (above), is unique, and never fails to charm visitors. Facing page: dense clouds blanket the redwood landscape.

Crater Lake (these pages), the focal point of Oregon's Crater Lake National Park, is the deepest lake in the U.S. The lake – which has neither an inlet nor an outlet – was formed as rain water and snow melt collected in the enormous basin left following the explosion of Mount Mazama over 6,000 years ago. Wizard Island (facing page), a conical, black cinder cone, is the largest of the islands on the lake.

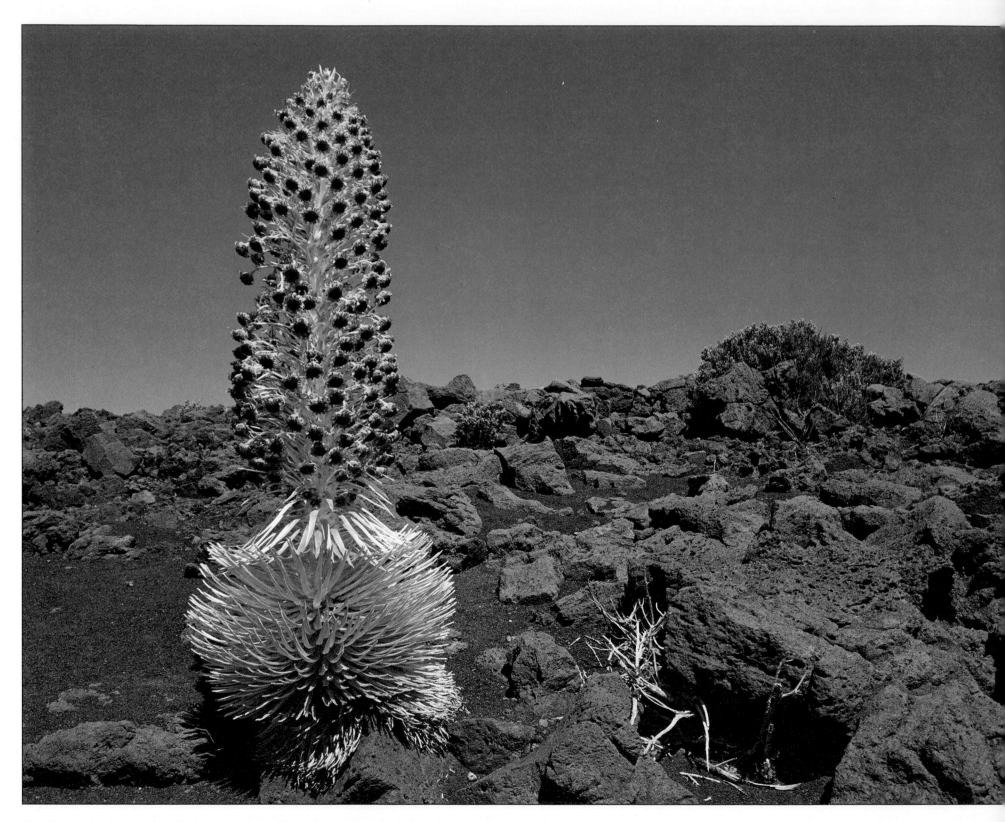

World-famous Haleakala volcano (facing page), in Haleakala National Park on the Hawaiian island of Maui, is the world's largest dormant volcanic crater. The rare silversword (above), which grows for some twenty years and dies once it has produced its bloom, is found only in the park.

The summit of Mauna Kea, the largest of Hawaii Island's five volcanoes and the centerpiece of Hawaii Volcanoes National Park, rises above its mantle of cloud (above). Devastation Trail (facing page), a half mile of boardwalk leading through Hawaii Volcanoes, traverses its barren, almost ghostly landscape of tree skeletons and black ash.

Aside from Wind Cave itself, one of the main attractions of South Dakota's Wind Cave National Park are the bison herds (above), which roam the plains undisturbed. Facing page: rugged North Dakota terrain, in Theodore Roosevelt National Park.

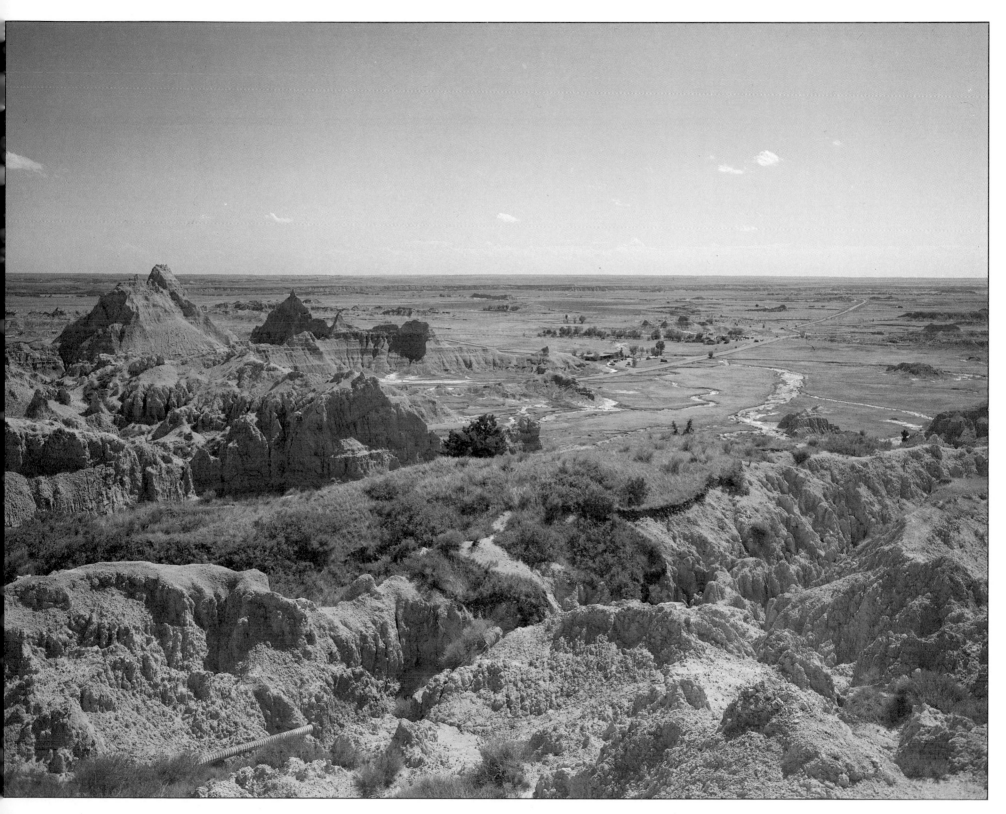

Badlands National Park (these pages), which lies between the Cheyenne and White rivers of South Dakota, was established as a monument in 1939, but did not receive full national park status until 1978. The park's spectacular, though forbidding, landscape is famous for its great fossil resources.

The mighty Grand Tetons (these pages), in Grand Teton National Park, Wyoming, tower over the surrounding flatlands. At night, the dramatic silhouettes of the jagged, saw-toothed peaks can be seen over the twilight waters of Snake River at Oxbow Bend (facing page). Overleaf: (left) Jackson Lake, and (right) snow-covered sagebrush flats at Jackson Hole, Grand Teton National Park.

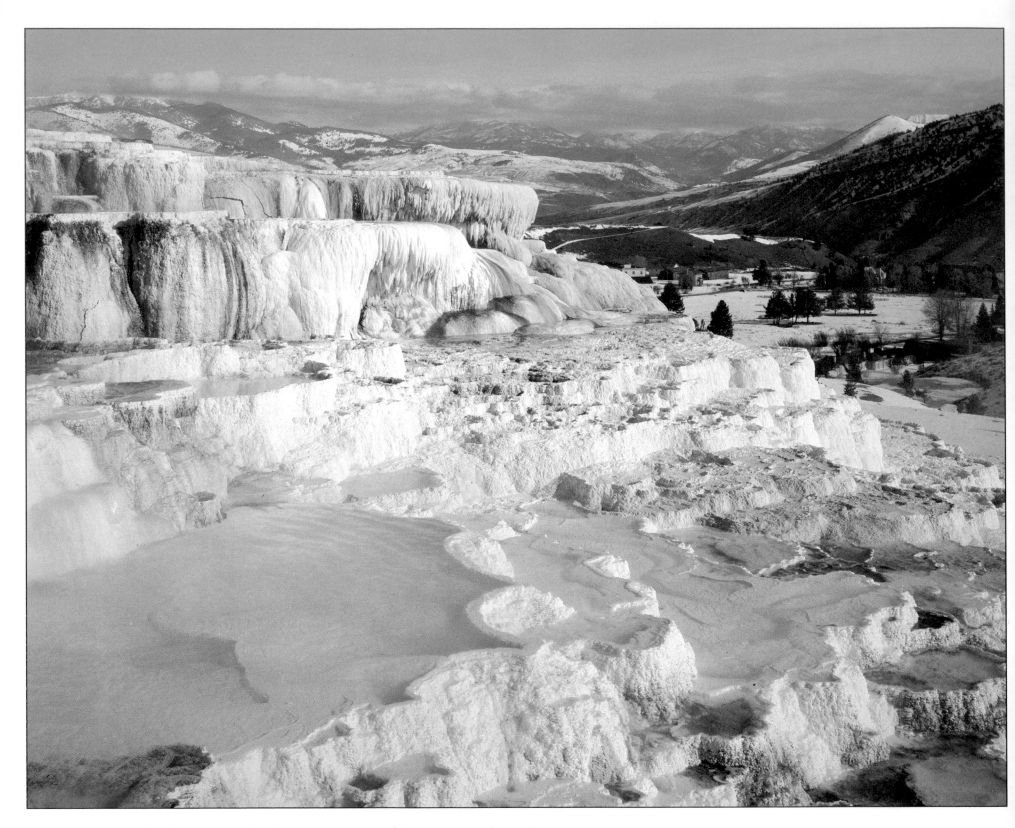

Yellowstone National Park (these pages), which covers an area of 3,500 square miles in the northwestern corner of Wyoming, is renowned as the world's greatest geyser area. The magical calcium carbonate creations of Minerva Terrace (above) at Mammoth Hot Spring, and the magnificent Morning Glory Pool (facing page) are just two of the park's attractions.

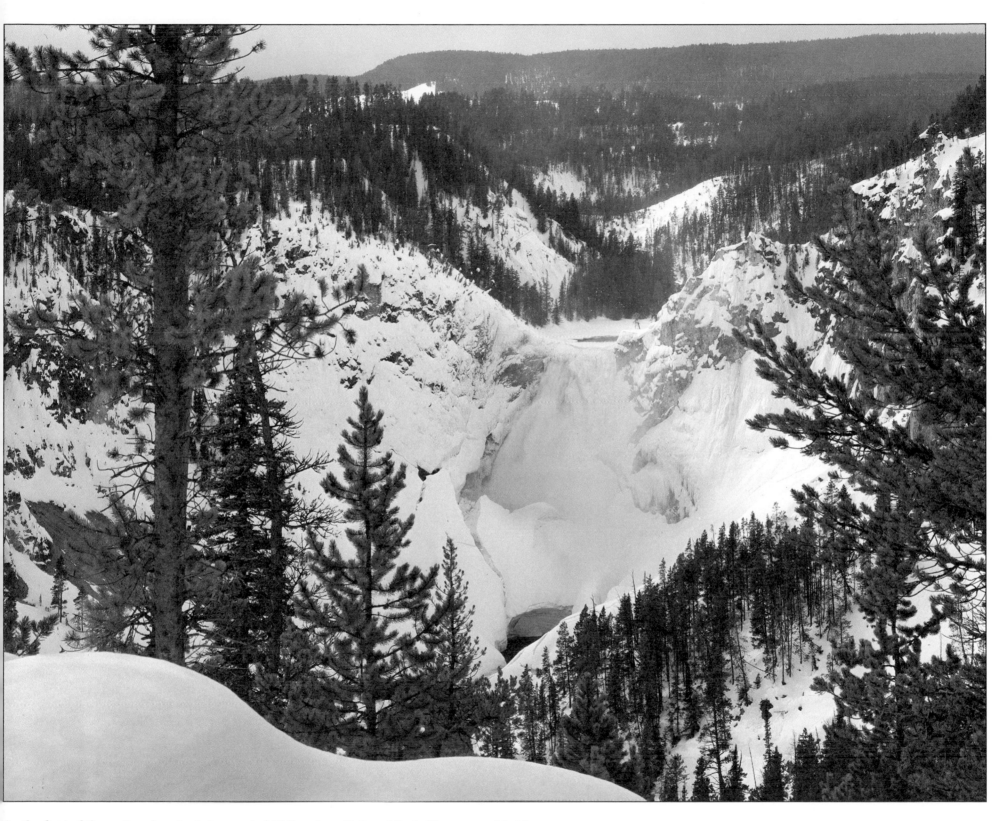

As the first of the national parks to be created, Yellowstone National Park (these pages) holds a special place in the nation's heart. The Lower Falls (above) and the Upper Falls (facing page) in the Grand Canyon of the Yellowstone River, are particularly noted for their beauty in all seasons.

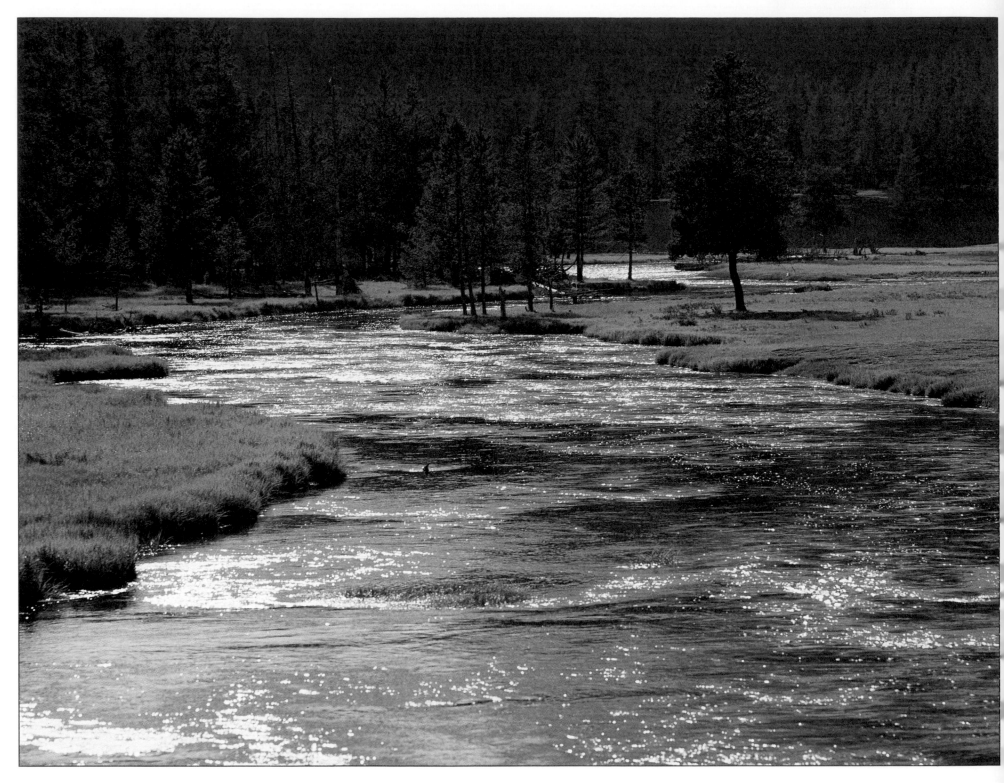

Above: the sparkling, silver ribbon of the Gibbon River, Yellowstone National Park. Facing page:
Firehole River, curving through Wyoming's steaming Midway Geyser Basin.

The wild mountain landscape of northern Montana has been preserved in Glacier National Park (these pages). The climate here is harsh, and snow remains on the higher peaks even in the height of summer. Two Medicine Lake (above) and St. Mary Lake (facing page) are two of the most beautiful and serene areas of the park.

Mount Rainier (facing page), the highest mountain in Washington State and the focal point of Mount Rainier National Park, is covered in snow and ice year round. The face of this now-dormant volcano is constantly, though gradually, being changed by the numerous glaciers that cover its surface. In spring and summer the subalpine meadows that surround the mountain are covered by colorful wildflowers. Above: pine-circled Bench Lake.

Aerial views lend the jagged, glacier-strewn peaks of the Cascade Range (these pages), in Washington State's North Cascades National Park, a still more forbidding aspect. Overleaf: Picture Lake, lying in the shadow of Mount Chuksan's mighty bulk.

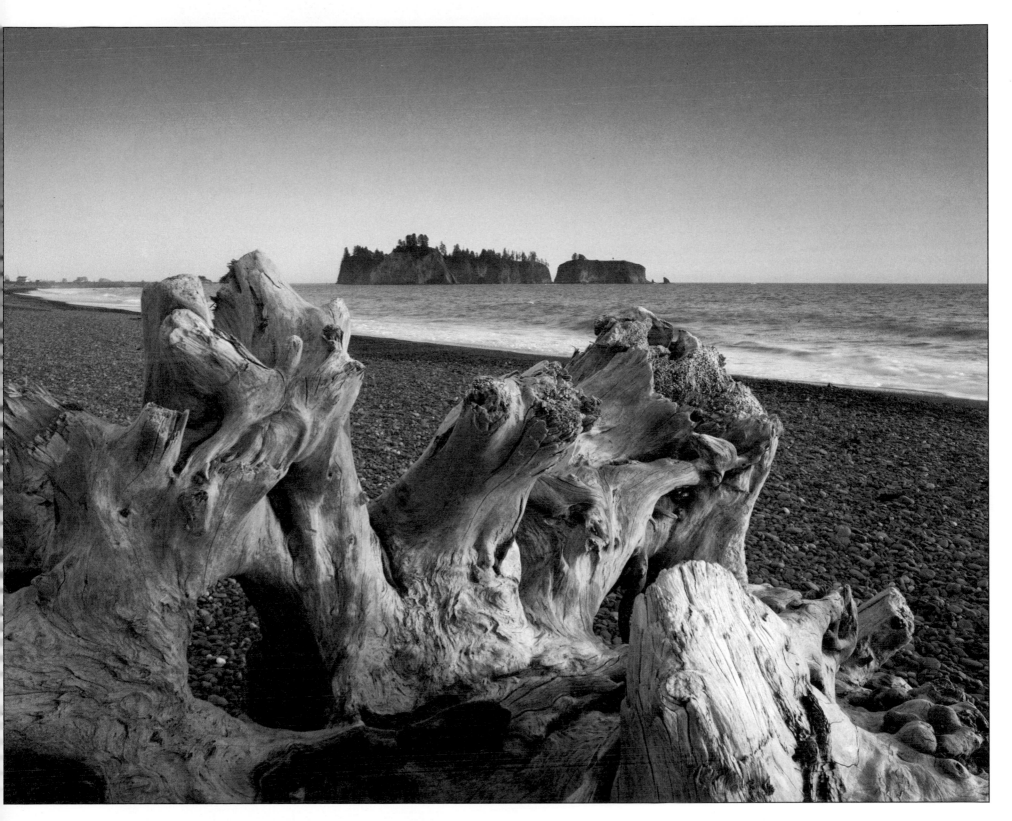

The remains of a once-mighty tree lies on Rialto Beach (above), on the Pacific coast of Olympic National Park, in Washington State. Facing page: boats skim the sunlit surface of the Hood Canal. Overleaf: a peaceful sunset on Big Bend, Hood Canal, Olympic National Park.